Close Reading with Paired Texts

Secondary

Engaging Lessons to Improve Comprehension

Authors
Lori Oczkus, M.A.
Timothy Rasinski, Ph.D.

Publishing Credits

Corinne Burton, M.A.Ed., *Publisher*; Conni Medina, M.A.Ed., *Managing Editor*; Emily R. Smith, M.A.Ed., *Content Director*; Shaun N. Bernadou, *Art Director*; Bianca Marchese, M.S. Ed., *Editor*; Jess Johnson, *Graphic Designer*; Stephanie Bernard, *Associate Editor*

Image Credits

p.21 Library of Congress [LC-USZ62-112728]; p.22 Library of Congress [LC-USZ62-5513]; p.25 Tony Baggett/Shutterstock; p.48 Don Johnston_ON/Alamy; p.76 Library of Congress [LC-USZ62-45818]; p.111 Library of Congress [LC-USW33-038546-ZC]; p.114 Library of Congress [LC-DIG-ppmsca-08407]; p.115 Library of Congress [LC-USZ62-93852]; all other images iStock and/or Shutterstock

Standards

© 2004 Mid-continent Research for Education and Learning (McREL)
© 2007 Teachers of English to Speakers of Other Languages, Inc. (TESOL)
© 2007 Board of Regents of the University of Wisconsin System. World-Class Instructional Design and Assessment (WIDA)
© Copyright 2010. National Governors Association Center for Best Practices and Council of Chief State School Officers. All rights reserved. (CCSS)
© Copyright 2007–2018 Texas Education Association (TEA). All rights reserved.

Shell Education
5301 Oceanus Drive
Huntington Beach, CA 92649-1030
www.tcmpub.com/shell-education
ISBN 978-1-4258-1735-0
© 2018 Shell Educational Publishing, Inc.

The classroom teacher may reproduce copies of materials in this book for classroom use only. The reproduction of any part for an entire school or school system is strictly prohibited. No part of this publication may be transmitted, stored, or recorded in any form without written permission from the publisher.

Website addresses included in this book are public domain and may be subject to changes or alterations of content after publication of this product. Shell Education does not take responsibility for the future accuracy or relevance and appropriateness of website addresses included in this book. Please contact the company if you come across any inappropriate or inaccurate website addresses, and they will be corrected in product reprints.

Table of Contents

Introduction
    About Close Reading 4

How to Use This Book
    Lesson Plan Overview 8

Language Arts Texts
    Unit 1—Beauty 10
    Unit 2—Mark Twain 19
    Unit 3—Monster Movies 28

Mathematics Texts
    Unit 4—Geometry 37
    Unit 5—Fractals 46
    Unit 6—Cryptography 55

Science Texts
    Unit 7—Engineering and Technology 64
    Unit 8—Radiation 73
    Unit 9—Stress 82

Social Studies Texts
    Unit 10—Equal Rights 91
    Unit 11—Women's Suffrage 100
    Unit 12—The Devastation of War 109

Appendices
    Appendix A: References Cited 118
    Appendix B: Correlation to the Standards 119
    Appendix C: Tips for Implementing the Lessons 122
    Appendix D: Strategies 123
    Appendix E: Assessment Options 125
    Appendix F: Student Reproducibles 126

About Close Reading

What Is Close Reading?

Students today need to carry a "tool kit" of effective reading strategies to help them comprehend a wide variety of texts. Close reading is one way for students to enhance their understanding, especially as they read more challenging texts. The Common Core State Standards (2010) call for students to "read closely to determine what the text says explicitly and to make logical inferences from it and cite specific textual evidence when writing or speaking to support conclusions drawn from the text." Instead of skipping or glossing over difficult texts, students need to develop strategies for digging into the text on their own (Fisher and Frey 2012). Good readers dig deeper as they read and reread a text for a variety of important purposes. Close reading involves rereading to highlight, underline, reconsider points, ask and answer questions, consider author's purpose and word choice, develop appropriate oral expression and fluency, and discuss the text with others. In close reading lessons, students learn to exercise the discipline and concentration for analyzing the text at hand rather than heading off topic. Students of all ages can be taught to carefully reread challenging texts on their own for a variety of purposes.

> Close reading involves rereading to highlight, underline, reconsider points, ask and answer questions, consider author's purpose and word choice, develop appropriate oral expression and fluency, and discuss the text with others.

Reciprocal Teaching, or the □Fab Four,□ and Close Reading

Reciprocal teaching is a scaffolded discussion technique that involves four of the most critical comprehension strategies that good readers employ to comprehend text—**predict**, **clarify**, **question**, and **summarize** (Oczkus 2010; Palincsar and Brown 1986). We refer to the reciprocal teaching strategies as "The Fab Four" (Oczkus 2012). These strategies may be discussed in any order but must all be included in every lesson. Together, the four strategies form a powerful package that strengthens comprehension. Research has found that students who engage in reciprocal teaching show improvement in as little as 15 days (Palincsar and Brown 1986) by participating more eagerly in discussions. After just three to six months, they may grow one to two years in their reading levels (Rosenshine and Meister 1994; Hattie 2008).

The reciprocal teaching strategies make it a practical lesson pattern for close readings. First, students briefly glance over a text to anticipate and predict the author's purpose, topic or theme, and text organization. As students read, they make note of words or phrases they want to clarify. During questioning, students reread to ask and answer questions and provide evidence from the text. Finally, students reread again to summarize and respond to the text. Quick partner and team cooperative discussions throughout the process increase students' comprehension and critical thinking. A strong teacher think-aloud component also pushes student thinking and provides students the modeling and support they need to learn to read challenging texts on their own. The four strategies become the tool kit students rely on as they read any text closely.

About Close Reading (cont.)

What Is Reading Fluency?

Fluency refers to the ability to read and understand the words encountered in texts accurately and automatically or effortlessly (Rasinski 2010). All readers come to a text with a limited or finite amount of cognitive resources. If they have to use too much of their cognitive resources to decode the words in the text, they have less of these resources available for the more important task in reading—comprehension. Readers who are not automatic in word recognition are easy to spot. They read text slowly and laboriously, often stopping at difficult words to figure them out. Although they may be able to accurately read the words, their comprehension suffers because too much of their attention had to be devoted to word recognition and away from comprehension. So although accuracy in word recognition is good, it is not enough. Fluency also includes automaticity. Good readers are fluent readers.

Fluency also has another component. It is prosody, or expressive reading. Fluent readers read orally with expression and phrasing that reflect and enhance the meaning of the passage (Rasinski 2010). Research has demonstrated that readers who are accurate, automatic, and expressive in their oral reading tend to be readers who read orally *and* silently with good comprehension. Moreover, students who perform poorly on tests of silent reading comprehension exhibit difficulties in one or more areas of reading fluency.

Fluency and Close Reading

How does a person become fluent? The simple answer is practice. However, there are various forms of practice in reading that nurture fluency in students. Students need to hear and talk about fluent reading from and with more proficient readers. In doing so, they develop an understanding of what actually constitutes fluent reading.

Fluency should be an essential part of close reading. Without some degree of fluency, it is difficult for students to successfully engage in close reading. If readers have to invest too much cognitive energy into the lower-level tasks of word recognition, they will have less energy available for the tasks required of close reading—interpreting author's purpose, noting detailed information, making inferences, etc. Close reading, by definition, requires readers to read a text more than once for different purposes. Reading a text more than once is called *repeated reading*. Moreover, one of the purposes for repeated reading can and should be to read a passage with a level of fluency that reflects the meaning of the text (Rasinski and Griffith 2010). For fluency strategies to use with students, see page 124.

> By combining close reading using reciprocal teaching strategies with fluency, we end up with greater reading benefits for students than if close reading and fluency were taught and practiced separately. It is simply more efficient, more effective, and more authentic to deal with both of these critical competencies together. We call it *synproval*. Your students will call it *fun*!

About Close Reading (cont.)

Why Pair Fiction and Nonfiction Texts?

Standards point out that from the initial stages of literacy development, students need exposure to both fiction and nonfiction texts. Yet the previous conventional wisdom was to focus primarily on fiction and gradually move toward more nonfiction. We provide a balance of the two texts throughout this book. In doing so, we give students opportunities to explore and gain proficiency in close reading strategies with a range of text types.

When pairing texts, we also provide a content connection between them. One passage can help build background knowledge, while the other passage focuses on building interest. Our paired texts allow students to engage in comparing and contrasting various types of texts, which in itself is a form of close reading.

The pairing of texts also helps students see that different forms of texts may require different levels or types of reading fluency. Fiction, including poetry, is written with voice. Authors and poets try to embed a voice in their writing that they wish the reader to hear. Texts written with voice should be read with expression. Thus, these texts lend themselves extremely well to reading with appropriate fluency. While nonfiction may also be written with voice, it is a different type of writing that often requires a different form of expression and fluency. By pairing these forms of texts, we offer students opportunities to master fluent reading in two forms.

Since multiple reading encounters with the same text are required in close reading activities, you will notice the texts are not very long. Students will be able to reread the engaging texts for multiple purposes to achieve greater success with their comprehension of the texts.

Close Reading and Differentiation

The close reading lessons in this resource are filled with many options for scaffolding to meet the needs of all students, including English language learners and struggling readers. The lessons offer a variety of stopping points, where the teacher can choose to think aloud and provide specific modeling, coaching, and feedback. Understanding your students' background knowledge and interests will help you decide whether you should read the informational texts first or grab students' interests by starting with the fictional texts. Throughout the lessons, vocabulary is addressed in a variety of creative ways that will help students who struggle to better understand the text. Sentence frames, such as *I think I will learn _____ because_____* or *I didn't get the word _____, so I _____*, provide students with a focus for their rereading tasks and discussions with peers. Creative options for rereading the texts to build fluency and comprehension give students who need more support lots of meaningful practice.

About Close Reading (cont.)

Effective Tips for Close Reading Lessons

To make the most out of close reading lessons, be sure to include the following:

1. **Text Focus**

   Throughout the lessons, keep the main focus on the text itself by examining how it is organized, the author's purpose, text evidence, and reasons why the author chose certain words or visuals.

2. **Think Alouds**

   Model close reading using teacher think alouds to help make thinking visible to students. For example, before asking students to find words to clarify, demonstrate by choosing a word from the text and showing different ways to clarify it.

3. **Cooperative Learning**

   Students' comprehension increases when they discuss the reading with others. Ask partners or groups to "turn and talk" during every step of the lesson.

4. **Scaffolding**

   Some students need extra support with comprehension or fluency. Use the suggestions on pages 123–124 that include sentence frames, ways to reread the text, props, gestures, and other ideas to reach every learner and make the lessons engaging.

5. **Metacognition/Independence**

   Name the rereading steps for students throughout the lessons. This will help them remember how to read closely when they encounter rigorous texts on their own. For example, before questioning say, "Now let's reread the text to find evidence as we ask and answer our questions."

   Adapted from Lori D. Oczkus (2018)

A Close Reading Snapshot

Below is an example showing what one lesson might look like.

> Mrs. Chen passes out the informational text about storms. Students participate in a quick and quiet text walk to anticipate the author's purpose and the topic. As students read the text silently, they circle words that are related to weather. Mrs. Chen reads aloud once through, modeling fluency. The students reread the text in small teams as they underline challenging words and ideas that they want to clarify. Using evidence from the text, students compare and contrast convection air in hurricanes and tornadoes. Then, students work in groups to create digital presentations of what they learned from the text.

Lesson Plan Overview

Teacher Pages

The lessons have overview pages that include summaries of the themes students will focus on and answer keys. Each lesson includes two Teacher Notes charts, one for the nonfiction text and one for the fiction text. Both charts follow the same structure as below. **Note:** You will find some teacher modeling suggestions in the right hand columns of the charts. Prior to implementing the lessons, provide students with copies of the texts to mark throughout the lessons, and project larger versions of the texts for the class to see so that you can model important steps in the close-reading process. You can find digital copies of the texts at **www.tcmpub.com/teachers/paired-texts/**.

Lesson Steps	Purpose
Ready, Set, Predict!	In this section, students will: • skim the text • anticipate the topic • think about the author's purpose • think about text organization
Go!	In this section, students will: • read the text independently • anticipate the topic • think about the author's purpose • think about text organization • listen to the teacher read the text aloud • reread the text for various purposes • focus on various aspects of fluency
Reread to Clarify	In this section, students will: • work independently, in pairs, or in small groups to reread the text and identify words or phrases they want to clarify • use various clarifying strategies such as sounding out, studying word parts, visualizing content, and rereading
Reread to Question	In this section, students will: • work independently, in pairs, or in small groups to reread the text and ask and answer questions about the text • use text evidence to answer questions that are self-generated or asked by the teacher
Reread to Summarize and Respond	In this section, students will: • work independently, in pairs, or in small groups to reread the text and summarize the main ideas and details • evaluate the text • share text evidence to support their summaries of the text

Lesson Plan Overview (cont.)

Student Pages

After reading each pair of fiction and nonfiction texts, the lesson plan continues with opportunities for comparing the two texts and creative follow-up options that can be conducted with the whole class, small groups, partners, or as independent work in a center.

Response Pages

Each text has a follow-up activity page where students use their knowledge of the text to answer text-dependent questions.

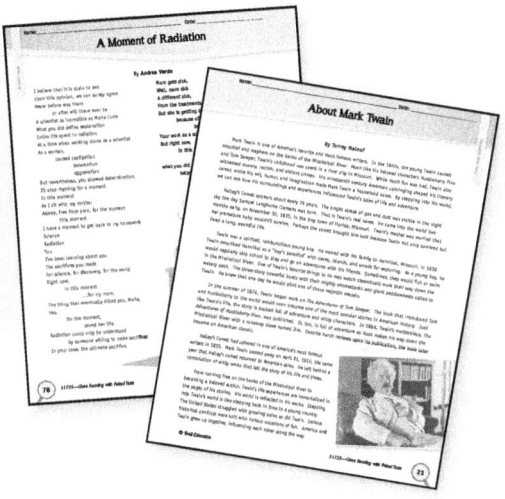

Comparing the Texts

This activity page offers creative opportunities for students to reread both texts and synthesize information from both to accomplish a task. A few examples include: composing a blog post, writing a tweet, or filling in a graphic organizer.

All About the Content

This page offers four extension activities that students can choose from that focus on their comprehension of the paired texts. The activities have the same focus in each lesson: reading, fluency, vocabulary, and writing.

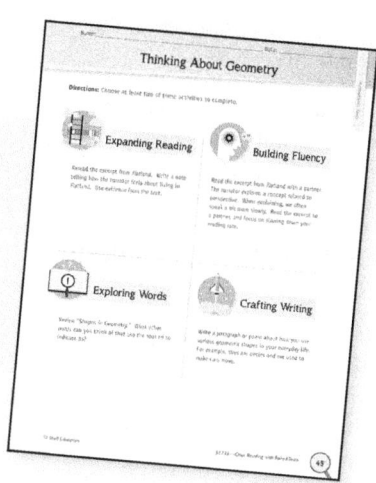

© Shell Education   51735—Close Reading with Paired Texts   9

Unit 1 Overview
Beauty

Theme Summary

Beauty is in the eye of the beholder—or is it? Actually, beauty is a very complex concept. It means different things to different people. With this text pair, students will learn that people all over the world are willing to do some pretty crazy things to achieve their definition of beauty. They will also read a poem that will have them asking, "Is trying to be beautiful really worth it?"

Answer Key

"Things We Do for Beauty" Response (page 13)

1. C. perception
2. Koreans clean away dirt from the day with two different cleansers. Then, they use essence to hydrate the skin and reduce wrinkles. After essence, they use a sheet mask for vitamins. Finally, they eat kimchi, a fermented cabbage, for a clear complexion.
3. Defining beauty is complex because each culture has a different idea about what beautiful means.
4. The author wants us to understand that our character, passion, and values add to our beauty as a person.

"Beauty Is Vain" Response (page 16)

1. B. think very highly of
2. The roses and lilies are described as red, white, sweet, and straight.
3. The author means that no matter how beautiful we are, we will all die eventually.
4. The author communicates that no matter what a person does to be beautiful, time eventually wins and we all age.

Let's Compare! Only Skin Deep (page 17)

Students' letters will vary but should include information about surprising hair and skincare practices, how chasing after beauty is vain, and the real meaning of being beautiful.

Standards

- Cite specific textual evidence to support analysis of primary and secondary sources.
- Determine the central ideas or information of a primary or secondary source; provide an accurate summary of the source distinct from prior knowledge or opinions.

Materials

- *Things We Do for Beauty* (page 12)
- *"Things We Do for Beauty" Response* (page 13)
- *Beauty Is Vain* (page 15)
- *"Beauty Is Vain" Response* (page 16)
- *Let's Compare! Only Skin Deep* (page 17)
- *Thinking About Beauty* (page 18)

Comparing the Texts

After students complete the lessons for each text, have them work in pairs to reread both texts and complete *Let's Compare! Only Skin Deep* (page 17). Finally, students can work to complete the *Thinking About Beauty!* matrix (page 18). The matrix activities allow students to work on important literacy skills of reading, writing, vocabulary, and fluency. For further text analysis, compare these texts to the fifth stanza of "13 Ways of Looking at a Blackbird" by Wallace Stevens.

Nonfiction Text Teacher Notes

Things We Do for Beauty

		Lesson Steps	Teacher Think Alouds
	Ready, Set, Predict!	• Tell students they will read a nonfiction text about the surprising things people do to be beautiful. • Have students pair up to think about commercials and advertisements they have seen about beauty products. Have them list the claims made and what the products are supposed to do. • Have students skim the headings in the text and predict what the text might be about. Encourage student pairs to share their predictions.	"I remember seeing a commercial on TV for a facial mask that was made with snails! I can't even imagine using mashed up snails on my face."
	Go!	• Provide the text for students, and display a larger version for the class to see while you model. • Have students read the text independently and underline any words or concepts that are unclear or that need clarification. • Read the text aloud, modeling fluent reading. Point out to students the importance of reading with accuracy.	
	Reread to Clarify	• Have students reread the text to clarify anything confusing. • Have students revisit the words or concepts they underlined to clarify their understanding. Then, have students share what they were able to clarify in small groups.	"In the section about sheet masks, it refers to *treasure troves*. I can keep reading to try to clarify the meaning. There's a clue in the text. So maybe a *treasure trove* is a valuable hidden treasure."
	Reread to Question	• Have students reread in pairs to identify portions of the text to write questions about. Have students work together, reading through the text again to find text evidence that answers their questions. • Have students respond to the questions and prompts on page 13.	"After reading the part about the 10-step skincare routine, I ask, 'How can there be so many steps in taking care of skin?' I find several of those steps in the text, so I'll underline them."
	Reread to Summarize and Respond	• Instruct students to reread the text to summarize. Have them identify the author's main idea, a few examples to support the main idea, and a final statement about the main idea. You may have students use different colors (highlighters or colored pencils) to help them find the main idea and details. • Have students meet in pairs to share their summaries.	"Before I write my summary, I'll review the text again. I will circle the main idea, underline some examples of surprising beauty practices, and underline part of the last paragraph that summarizes the text."

*Note: For more tips, engagement strategies, and fluency options to include in this lesson, see pages 122–128.

Things We Do for Beauty

By Monika Davies

People have done some pretty surprising things in the name of beauty. Glance through any style magazine, and you'll find no lack of creative beauty routines to try. In some places, beauty fanatics have smeared their faces with dehydrated bird droppings!

Beauty itself is a weird idea. The perception of beauty, of course, varies from person to person and culture to culture. Our idea of beauty reflects our lifestyle and values. Learning more about another culture's interpretation of what makes people beautiful gives meaningful insight into that culture's way of life.

Digging into Makeup Bags

Examining a makeup bag from another country is a fascinating glimpse into a lifestyle different from one's own. Let's take a look to see what people have tucked into their cosmetic totes in Korea.

Korea

Many Koreans take pride in having flawless complexions, a direct result of a 10-step (yes, 10!) skincare routine. The process begins with an oil-based cleanser, followed with a foaming cleanser. Koreans are gentle with their faces, using circular motions to cleanse a day's grime away.

Uniquely Korean, essence is a highly concentrated liquid. Full of beneficial properties, such as glycerin, essence hydrates your skin. A staple in the Asian beauty regimen, essence is said to promote a wrinkle free complexion.

While sheet masks can make you look like a mummy, Koreans swear by this unique skin-care solution. Sheet masks are treasure troves of skin-friendly vitamins. Letting the mask settle on your face allows the vitamins to absorb, ideally giving you the glow that's advertised!

The famous saying "you are what you eat" is also a part of Korean skin care. Kimchi is a beloved Korean superfood. This spicy fermented cabbage is loaded with antioxidants, which create a clear complexion.

Complex Beauty

Defining beauty is complex and will always be subject to scrutiny. Things that seem surprising to some people aren't strange to others or out of place within a given culture. Each culture defines "beautiful" differently. Every culture, country, and person has different approaches to demonstrating beauty. Undoubtedly, beauty is a concept with many definitions. Those definitions change over the years, with new trends setting in. In a world of selfies and social media, it's even more important to focus on what can't be seen. Make sure your concept of beauty encompasses your character, your passion, and your values. And keep in mind that every person's definition of what makes someone beautiful grows and evolves with time. In the end, the most meaningful perspective will always be the one we determine for ourselves.

Name:_____ Date:_____

▢Things We Do for Beauty▢ Response

Directions: Reread the text on page 12 to answer each question.

1. What does the author say varies from person to person and culture to culture?

   Ⓐ products   Ⓒ perception

   Ⓑ creativity   Ⓓ looks

2. Summarize the beauty routine and purposes of products in Korea.
   _____
   _____
   _____
   _____

3. Why do you think defining beauty is complex?
   _____
   _____
   _____
   _____

4. Why does the author suggest focusing on what can't be seen?
   _____
   _____
   _____
   _____

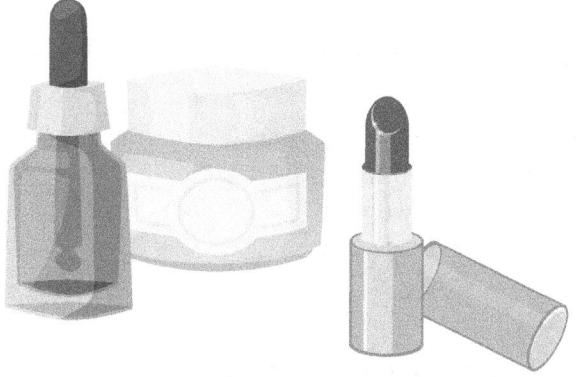

Fiction Text Teacher Notes
Beauty Is Vain

	Lesson Steps	Teacher Think Alouds
Ready, Set, Predict!	• Provide students with the poem, and display a larger version for the class to see while you model. • Have students read the title and determine the meaning of the word *vain*. If they have trouble with the meaning, explain that the definition is "being overly concerned about appearance." • Ask students to glance at the poem. What do they think it will be about? What can they tell from the format and structure of the poem and the way it looks? What predictions can they make about it?	
Go!	• Have students read the poem independently, underlining unfamiliar, descriptive, or interesting words in the poem. • Read the text aloud as students follow along. Discuss the theme of beauty and the author's thoughts about it. Have students notice the rhythm that is embedded in the poem.	
Reread to Clarify	• Have students reread the poem to clarify by visualizing. Instruct them to circle portions of the text that help them to picture the flowers. • Have students meet in pairs to discuss the text they circled and what it communicates about beauty.	"I have to clarify and reread the part where the author compares a woman's beauty to flowers. She says that a woman can do things to be beautiful, but that these things will not make her any more beautiful than flowers."
Reread to Question	• Tell students to reread the text for the purpose of questioning. Have them share their questions with partners and find clues in the text to answer them. Provide sentence starters if students are having a difficult time developing questions. What is the author saying about… Why do you think… I wonder why…	"When I read the first stanza, I ask, 'What is the author saying about the woman compared to the flowers?' Then, I realize she is saying that a woman can never be *more* beautiful than a flower."
Reread to Summarize and Respond	• Have partners work together to summarize the main message of the poem, in particular, focusing on the message the author communicates in the second stanza. Have students jot five key words from the poem to summarize to main message from the poem.	"When I summarize the poem, it helps me to think about the main message."

*****Note:** For more tips, engagement strategies, and fluency options to include in this lesson, see pages 122–128.

Beauty Is Vain

by Christina Georgina Rossetti

While roses are so red,
    While lilies are so white,
Shall a woman exalt her face
    Because it gives delight?
She's not so sweet as a rose,
    A lily's straighter than she,
And if she were as red or white
    She'd be but one of three.

Whether she flush in love's summer
    Or in its winter grow pale,
Whether she flaunt her beauty
    Or hide it away in a veil,
Be she red or white,
    And stand she erect or bowed,
Time will win the race he runs with her
    And hide her away in a shroud.

Name:_____ Date:_____

"Beauty Is Vain" Response

Directions: Reread the text on page 15 to answer each question.

1. In the first stanza, what is the meaning of the word *exalt*?

   Ⓐ be discouraged about   Ⓒ try very hard

   Ⓑ think very highly of   Ⓓ accept something as it is

2. How does the author describe the roses and lilies?

   _____
   _____
   _____
   _____

3. What is the meaning of the last two lines of the poem?

   _____
   _____
   _____
   _____

4. What is the message the author communicates about what time will do?

   _____
   _____
   _____
   _____

Name:_____ Date:_____

Let's Compare!
Only Skin Deep

Directions: As the saying goes, "Beauty is only skin deep." It means that real beauty comes from the inside. Reread both texts. Use information from both texts to help you write an advice letter to a preteen girl or boy about the meaning of beauty. Describe some of the crazy things people do to try to be beautiful. End your letter with a message about what real beauty is.

Dear _____ ,
       (name)

_____
_____
_____
_____
_____
_____
_____
_____
_____
_____
_____
_____
_____
_____
_____
_____
_____
_____

Sincerely,

_____

Name: _____ Date: _____

Thinking About Beauty

Directions: Choose at least two of these activities to complete.

 ## Expanding Reading

Reread "Things We Do for Beauty." Highlight a part of the text that tells of the beauty practice you find to be the most surprising. Do a quick online search about this beauty practice. Write what you find in the margins of the text.

 ## Building Fluency

Read "Beauty Is Vain" with a partner. Pay close attention to punctuation and pauses indicated by commas or the ends of lines. Practice reading with appropriate rhythm, pauses, and voice inflections. For example, your voice should go up slightly when reading the line with the question mark. Perform the poem with a partner. Each partner will read two lines at a time.

 ## Exploring Words

Create a list of at least ten words that are synonyms for *beauty*. Then make a list of at least five synonyms for *vain* or *vanity*. Write an original saying about beauty and/or vanity using some of the words you find.

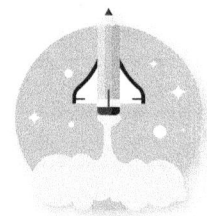 ## Crafting Writing

"Beauty is in the eye of the beholder" and "Beauty is only skin deep" are well-known sayings about beauty. Search online for "beauty sayings" or "beauty quotations." Make a list of five of your favorites. Write the intended message for each one.

Unit 2 Overview
Mark Twain

Theme Summary

Mark Twain is a famous American author best known for his books about Tom Sawyer and Huckleberry Finn. With this text pair, students will learn about Twain's life and experiences. They will also read an excerpt from one of Twain's famous works, *The Adventures of Tom Sawyer*.

Standards

- Determine a theme or central idea of a text and how it is conveyed through particular details.
- Engage effectively in a range of collaborative discussions.

Materials

- *About Mark Twain* (page 21)
- *"About Mark Twain" Response* (page 22)
- *Excerpt from* The Adventures of Tom Sawyer (pages 24)
- *Excerpt from* The Adventures of Tom Sawyer *Response* (page 25)
- *Let's Compare! Church Pinchbug in Verse* (page 26)
- *Thinking About Mark Twain* (page 27)

Comparing the Texts

After students complete the lessons for each text, have them work in pairs to reread both texts and complete *Let's Compare! Church Pinchbug in Verse* (page 26). Finally, students can work to complete the *Thinking About Mark Twain* matrix (page 27). The matrix activities allow students to work on important literacy skills of reading, writing, vocabulary, and fluency. For further text analysis, compare these texts to "Goodnight, Sweetheart, Goodnight" by Mark Twain.

Answer Key

"About Mark Twain" Response (page 22)

1. C. 76
2. The text says that Twain's books about Tom Sawyer and Huckleberry Finn became popular classics, but it says that *The Adventures of Huckleberry Finn* was his masterpiece. A masterpiece would mean it was his best work.
3. Tom and Huck probably explore caves, islands, and woods. The books might also include adventures near the Mississippi River with the boys fishing and swimming.

Excerpt from *The Adventures of Tom Sawyer* **Response** (page 25)

1. A. The preacher is boring.
2. D. The dog shouldn't have taken the bug with him.
3. The author gives the dog human characteristics. He says the dog feels foolish, has resentment in his heart, and wants revenge.
4. The author refers to the dog as the *frantic sufferer*. It means that the dog is panicked and in pain.

Let's Compare! Church Pinchbug in Verse (page 26)

Students' poems will vary. Here's an example:

Mark Twain is a humorous man. / Makes people laugh whenever he can. / He tells tale of a poodle / who lost his noodle, / and with that bug, how his efforts were futile!

Nonfiction Text Teacher Notes
About Mark Twain

	Lesson Steps	Teacher Think Alouds
Ready, Set, Predict!	• Tell students they will read a nonfiction text about Mark Twain. Have students work with partners to think, pair, share what they know about him. • Have students read the first sentence of each paragraph and predict what they will learn about Twain. Have students share their predictions in small groups. • Provide the text for students, and display a larger version for the class to see.	"Reading just the first sentences of each paragraph makes me a little confused. I don't understand why there is information about Halley's Comet. Maybe Twain liked to study astronomy."
Go!	• Have students read the text independently, circling any words or terminology they do not understand or find interesting. • Read the text aloud, modeling fluent reading. Have students take note of slight pauses in your reading when you encounter commas in the text.	
Reread to Clarify	• Have students reread the text, underlining anything confusing about the text. • Invite students to revisit the things they underlined and discuss them with pairs to clarify areas of confusion.	"After reading the part about Twain being born on the day Halley's Comet appeared, I wonder why that was in the text. Then, I realize that Halley's Comet appeared on the day he was born and on the day he died. That's pretty unusual."
Reread to Question	• Direct students to reread the text in pairs for the purpose of asking questions. Ask each student to write two questions that can be answered from the text. Pairs then ask each other their questions. Students should use evidence from the text in their answers. • Have students respond to the questions and prompts on page 22.	
Reread to Summarize and Respond	• Instruct students to reread the text to summarize. Have each student use different colors (highlighters or pencils) to draw a box around the main point of each paragraph. Students use the main point of each paragraph to write their summaries. • Have students meet in pairs to share their summaries.	"I'm going to underline the last sentence in the first paragraph because I think the main point is that Twain's experiences influenced his stories of life and adventure."

*****Note:** For more tips, engagement strategies, and fluency options to include in this lesson, see pages 122–128.

About Mark Twain

By Torrey Maloof

Mark Twain is one of America's favorite and most famous writers. In the 1840s, the young Twain caused mischief and mayhem on the banks of the Mississippi River. Much like his beloved characters Huckleberry Finn and Tom Sawyer, Twain's childhood was spent in a river city in Missouri. While much fun was had, Twain also witnessed slavery, racism, and violent crimes. His nineteenth century American upbringing shaped his literary career, while his wit, humor, and imagination made Mark Twain a household name. By stepping into his world, we can see how his surroundings and experiences influenced Twain's tales of life and adventure.

Halley's Comet appears about every 76 years. The bright streak of gas and dust was visible in the night sky the day Samuel Langhorne Clemens was born. That is Twain's real name. He came into the world two months early, on November 30, 1835, in the tiny town of Florida, Missouri. Twain's mother was worried that her premature baby wouldn't survive. Perhaps the comet brought him luck because Twain not only survived but lived a long, eventful life.

Twain was a spirited, rambunctious young boy. He moved with his family to Hannibal, Missouri, in 1839. Twain described Hannibal as a "boy's paradise" with caves, islands, and woods for exploring. As a young boy, he would regularly skip school to play and go on adventures with his friends. Sometimes, they would fish or swim in the Mississippi River. One of Twain's favorite things to do was watch steamboats work their way down the watery path. The three-story powerful boats with their mighty smokestacks and giant paddlewheels called to Twain. He knew that one day he would pilot one of those majestic vessels.

In the summer of 1874, Twain began work on *The Adventures of Tom Sawyer*. The book that introduced Tom and Huckleberry to the world would soon become one of the most popular stories in American history. Just like Twain's life, the story is packed full of adventure and witty characters. In 1884, Twain's masterpiece, *The Adventures of Huckleberry Finn*, was published. It, too, is full of adventure as Huck makes his way down the Mississippi River with a runaway slave named Jim. Despite harsh reviews upon its publication, the book later became an American classic.

Halley's Comet had ushered in one of America's most famous writers in 1835. Mark Twain passed away on April 21, 1910, the same year that Halley's comet returned to American skies. He left behind a compilation of witty works that tell the story of his life and times.

From running free on the banks of the Mississippi River to becoming a beloved author, Twain's life experiences are immortalized in the pages of his stories. His world is reflected in his works. Stepping into Twain's world is like stepping back in time to a young country. The United States struggled with growing pains as did Twain. Serious historical conflicts were knit with riotous occasions of fun. America and Twain grew up together, influencing each other along the way.

Name: _____ Date: _____

▢About Mark Twain▢ Response

Directions: Reread the text on page 21 to answer each question.

1. Based on clues in the text, about how many years did Mark Twain live?

   Ⓐ 89 Ⓒ 76

   Ⓑ 44 Ⓓ over 90

2. Which of Twain's books is considered his best, and how can you tell?
   _____
   _____
   _____

3. If the lives of Tom Sawyer and Huck Finn were based on Twain's life, what can you predict about some of the adventures Tom and Huck have in the books?
   _____
   _____
   _____
   _____
   _____

Twain in 1907

Fiction Text Teacher Notes

Excerpt from *The Adventures of Tom Sawyer*

	Lesson Steps	Teacher Think Alouds
Ready, Set, Predict!	• Provide students with the excerpt from *The Adventures of Tom Sawyer,* and display a larger version for the class to see while you model. • Have students read the title, skim the text, and predict the kinds of adventures Tom Sawyer has in the book. • Have students meet in pairs to talk about what the excerpt might reveal about Tom Sawyer's character.	
Go!	• Have students read the excerpt independently, underlining the author's use of humor. • Read the text aloud, modeling fluent reading. Draw attention to your use of appropriate reading rate. • Point out to students that we learn more about Twain's personality as we read this humorous event in the story.	"Twain uses detailed description, making it easy to visualize the scene. I can picture the dog's interactions with the pinchbug, the people hiding their laughter, and Tom's enjoyment of it all."
Reread to Clarify	• Have students reread the excerpt to clarify. Instruct them to circle examples of Twain's use of descriptive language. • Have students meet in pairs to discuss the text they circled and what it helps them to visualize.	"As I reread, I pay close attention to Twain's descriptive language. It says the people are *suffocating with suppressed laughter*. They want to laugh hard, but because they are in church, they try desperately not to laugh out loud."
Reread to Question	• Tell students to reread the text for the purpose of questioning. Have them share their questions with partners and determine whether the events reveal things about the time period of the story.	
Reread to Summarize and Respond	• Have partners work together to summarize the excerpt in drawings. Ask pairs to decide on what to include in their drawings to effectively summarize the excerpt or a part of the excerpt.	"When I think of summarizing the excerpt visually, I think of the scene I pictured in my mind—the church, the dog, the bug, the people, and a lot of chaos."

Note: For more tips, engagement strategies, and fluency options to include in this lesson, see pages 122–128.

Excerpt from *The Adventures of Tom Sawyer*

by Mark Twain

The minister droned monotonously through a sermon so boring that many a head began to nod. Presently Tom remembered a treasure he had and got out a percussion-cap box. In it was an enormous black beetle with formidable jaw—"pinchbug." The beetle seized his finger; Tom shook his hand, and the beetle went floundering into the aisle and lit on its back, and the injured finger went into the boy's mouth. The beetle lay there working its legs helplessly, unable to turn over. Tom eyed it, and longed for it; but it was out of his reach. Other people uninterested in the sermon also eyed the pinchbug.

Presently a poodle came idling along and spied the beetle; his drooping tail lifted and wagged. He surveyed the prize; walked around it; smelled it from a safe distance; walked around it again; grew bolder, and took a closer smell; then lifted his lip and made a gingerly snatch at it, just missing it; made another, and another; laid down on his stomach with the beetle between his paws, and continued his experiments; grew weary at last, and then indifferent and absent-minded. His head nodded, and little by little his chin descended until it touched the enemy, who seized it. There was a sharp yelp, a jerk of the poodle's head, and the pinchbug fell a couple of yards away, on its back once more. Neighboring spectators shook with gentle inward laughter, several faces rapidly went behind fans and handkerchiefs, and Tom was entirely happy. The dog looked foolish, and probably felt so; but there was resentment in his heart, too, and a craving for revenge, so he went to the pinchbug and began a wary attack on it again; jumping at it from every angle, landing with his forepaws within an inch of the creature, making ever closer snatches at it with his teeth, and shaking his head until his ears flapped.

But the poodle grew tired after a while; tried to amuse himself with a fly but found no relief; followed an ant around with his nose close to the floor and quickly wearied of that; yawned, sighed, forgot the pinchbug entirely, and sat down on it. With wild yelps of agony, the poodle went sailing up the aisle; he crossed the church in front of the altar; he flew down the other aisle; he crossed before the doors. At last the frantic sufferer veered from its course and sprang into its master's lap. Embarrassed, he flung it out an open window, and its yelps of distress quickly thinned and died in the distance.

By this time the whole congregation was red-faced and suffocating with suppressed laughter, and the sermon had come to an absolute standstill. Although the minister valiantly tried to restart, his words were received with a smothered burst of unholy mirth. It was a genuine relief to everyone in the congregation when the final blessing was pronounced.

Tom Sawyer went home cheerful, thinking to himself that there was satisfaction about religious service when there was variety to it. He had but one negative thought: He was willing that the dog should play with his pinchbug, but he did not think it was fitting for him to carry it off.

Name: _____ Date: _____

Excerpt from *The Adventures of Tom Sawyer* Response

Directions: Reread the text on page 24 to answer each question.

1. What does it mean that the preacher drones monotonously?

   Ⓐ The preacher is boring.   Ⓒ The preacher is mean.

   Ⓑ The preacher is loud.   Ⓓ The preacher is too quiet to hear.

2. What was Sawyer's negative thought?

   Ⓐ The sermon was boring.   Ⓒ The people shouldn't be laughing.

   Ⓑ The pinchbug shouldn't have pinched the dog.   Ⓓ The dog shouldn't have taken the bug with him.

3. How does the author personify the dog?

   _____
   _____
   _____

4. What phrase does the author use to describe the dog, and what does it mean?

   _____
   _____
   _____
   _____

Name: _____ Date: _____

Let's Compare!

Church Pinchbug in Verse

Directions: Reread both texts. Use information from both texts to help you write a poem about Mark Twain and his funny tale of the pinchbug in church. Begin by listing words about Twain and the excerpt in the box. Use many of the words in the poem you write. If possible, record yourself reading the poems.

Name: _____ Date: _____

Thinking About Mark Twain

Directions: Choose at least two of these activities to complete.

 ## Expanding Reading

 ## Building Fluency

Reread the text entitled, "Mark Twain." Highlight the part of the text that is most interesting to you. Write a note in the margin with your thoughts about the famous author. Be sure to include why you found that text the most interesting.

With a partner, practice reading the excerpt from *The Adventures of Tom Sawyer*. Take turns reading every other paragraph. Focus on the use of expression to make the text entertaining for listeners. Then, rehearse and perform your reading.

 ## Exploring Words

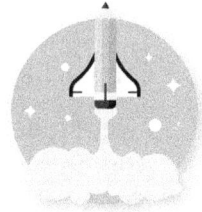 ## Crafting Writing

Create a list of at least ten descriptive words or phrases used by Twain in the excerpt from *The Adventures of Tom Sawyer*. Share your list with a partner, and discuss the visual images the words helped you create.

Write an acrostic poem about Twain. Write his name vertically down the left side of a sheet of paper. Use a word or phrase that describes Twain that begins with each letter of his name.

Unit 3 Overview
Monster Movies

Theme Summary

Monster movies have been around since the 1930s. From vampires and humans brought back to life to aliens and killer robots, movie monsters come in all forms. With new monster movies hitting the big screen almost every year, it seems that just about everyone loves a good scare.

Answer Key

"Monster Movie History" Response (page 31)

1. A. have changed over time

2. The text says that Frankenstein died at the end of the movie but there were more movies made about him. A sequel or reboot must mean that the story continues or a retelling of the story.

3. The movies have improved, and the content has changed. Monster movies will probably get scarier in the future and have better special effects.

Excerpt from *Frankenstein* Response (page 34)

1. B. He looks at the result of his hard work.

2. He says he *has miserably given life* to the corpse. Using the word *miserably* communicates that he wishes he had not done it.

3. Dr. Frankenstein cannot sleep. His heart is racing, he is weak and disappointed. His experiment did not turn out as planned, and his dreams are crushed.

Let's Compare! The Frankenstein Story (page 35)

Nonfiction: originally a book; many films come from the story; scientist's name was Dr. Frankenstein; monster dies in the movie

Both: Scientists bring a dead body to life.

Fiction: scientist is afraid of the monster; monster has yellow skin, watery eyes, black hair, and black lips; scientist is disappointed

Standards

⟶ Cite textual evidence to support analysis of what the text says explicitly as well as inferences drawn from the text.

⟶ Engage effectively in a range of collaborative discussions.

Materials

⟶ *Monster Movie History* (page 30)
⟶ *"Monster Movie History" Response* (page 31)
⟶ *Excerpt from* Frankenstein (page 33)
⟶ *Excerpt from* Frankenstein *Response* (page 34)
⟶ *Let's Compare! The Frankenstein Story* (page 35)
⟶ *Thinking About Monster Movies* (page 36)

Comparing the Texts

After students complete the lessons for each text, have them work in pairs to reread both texts and complete *Let's Compare! The Frankenstein Story* (page 35). Finally, students can work to complete the *Thinking About Monster Movies* matrix (page 36). The matrix activities allow students to work on important literacy skills of reading, writing, vocabulary, and fluency.

Nonfiction Text Teacher Notes
Monster Movie History

	Lesson Steps	Teacher Think Alouds
Ready, Set, Predict!	• Tell students they will read a nonfiction text about the history of monster movies. Ask students to think of what they know about monster movies and what they think the text might be about. Have them make lists of their thoughts and share them in groups. Students can do quick sketches of their favorite monsters. You may consider playing a movie trailer for an age-appropriate monster movie.	
Go!	• Provide the text for students, and display a larger version for the class to see while you model. • Have students read the text independently, underlining the main premise of each movie. Have them share in small groups. • Read the text aloud, modeling fluent reading. Point out your reading rate, explaining the importance of not reading too quickly or too slowly.	
Reread to Clarify	• Have students circle words or ideas in the text that they do not understand and share their thoughts with partners.	"If I don't understand the meaning of the word *evolved*, I can reread to clarify the word. The next sentence says monster movies have improved, so *evolved* means improved or changed."
Reread to Question	• Have students reread the text in pairs for the purpose of asking questions. Tell each student to write two questions about the text. Then, have pairs discuss the questions and answer them with evidence from the text. • Have students respond to the questions and prompts on page 31.	"After reading about the Dracula movie, I have a question: Why would people be so afraid that they passed out? The movie dates are evidence. Monster movies had not been around for long, so people were not used to movies like this."
Reread to Summarize and Respond	• Instruct students to reread the text to summarize. Have them draw stars beside main points and write sentences in the margin about the movie descriptions. Then, direct them to write summaries. • Have students meet in pairs to share their summaries.	"The first paragraph tells us that monster movies have a long history. I'm going to put a star beside that sentence because it is a good beginning for a summary."

*Note: For more tips, engagement strategies, and fluency options to include in this lesson, see pages 122–128.

Monster Movie History

By Timothy J. Bradley

The history of monster movies is a long and fascinating one. Many of us enjoy good, scary films. Monster movies have evolved since their beginnings. Improvements in filmmaking and technology have allowed for new creatures to exist and new stories to be told. So, grab that popcorn and a good friend to hide behind, and get ready to explore monster movies from the very beginning.

Frankenstein (1931)

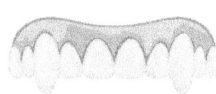

A very popular book that was adapted into a monster movie is *Frankenstein*. It tells of a scientist who jolts a dead human body back to life. The story sparked many films. The most popular one stars Boris Karloff as Dr. Frankenstein's monster. Even though the creature dies at the end of the film, his popularity lives on. There have been many sequels and reboots.

Dracula (1931)

The film follows the bloodthirsty vampire from his castle in Transylvania to London. The film terrified audiences. In fact, newspapers reported that several audience members passed out from fear!

Creature from the Black Lagoon (1954)

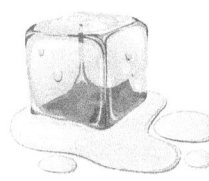

Creature from the Black Lagoon features a humanoid monster mutant who can survive underwater. The film tells the story of an archaeological expedition into the jungle. It attracts a curious gill man. The gill man wants to watch the explorers. But the creature frightens the humans. So, the humans attack him, but the gill man fights back.

The Thing (1982)

When *The Thing* opened in theaters, the ultra-gory effects stunned audiences. *The Thing* is about a shape-shifting alien astronaut frozen in Arctic ice. The staff of a scientific outpost thaws the alien. Then, it starts to mimic and kill the men one by one.

I, Robot (2004)

The film *I, Robot* tells the story of a police officer in Chicago. The movie takes place in the future. The officer investigates a suicide that might be a murder... committed by a robot. It's hard to imagine where moviemakers might go in the future. The advances that have been made so far suggest that even more amazing things are to come.

Name:_____ Date:_____

▫Monster Movie History▫ Response

Directions: Reread the text on page 30 to answer each question.

1. From the text, we learn that monster movies _____.

   Ⓐ have changed over time

   Ⓑ are not as scary as they once were

   Ⓒ are not as popular now as they used to be

   Ⓓ are going out of style

2. Use evidence in the text to determine the meaning of movie *sequels* and *reboots*.
   _____
   _____
   _____

3. What does the text tell you about how monster movies have changed over time? How do you think the next generation of monster movies will be different from the current ones? Why?
   _____
   _____
   _____
   _____

Fiction Text Teacher Notes
Excerpt from *Frankenstein*

	Lesson Steps	Teacher Think Alouds
Ready, Set, Predict!	• Provide students with the excerpt from *Frankenstein,* and display a larger version for the class to see while you model. • Ask students what they know about *Frankenstein*. Direct students to discuss with partners briefly and then read the title and predict what they might learn. • Have students meet in pairs to talk about their predictions.	"I know that Frankenstein is a scientist who brought a man back to life. That man turned into a monster. I wonder why being brought back to life made him a monster. I predict that the text will tell us more about the person's transformation."
Go!	• Have students read the excerpt independently, underlining the words that show the narrator's fear. • Read the text aloud as students follow along. Ask students to consider how the descriptions paint a spooky picture of the setting.	"The narrator (Dr. Frankenstein) tells us that it is raining, there is a candle in the room that is almost burned out, and it's one in the morning, so the room is dim. That seems very spooky to me."
Reread to Clarify	• Tell students to circle words that describe the monster. Encourage them to share how these words form a picture of Frankenstein's monster. • Have students meet in pairs to discuss the text they circled. Visualizing, or forming a picture in your mind, helps you to clarify what you're reading.	"When I reread the passage, I clarify in my mind how the monster looks. The narrator tells us this a lot, using the phrases *yellow skin* and *black lips*."
Reread to Question	• Tell students to reread the text for the purpose of questioning. Have them share their questions with partners.	"When the monster opens his eyes and reaches out, the scientist runs away. Doesn't he want to see the creature he worked so hard to create?"
Reread to Summarize and Respond	• Have partners work together to summarize the excerpt by drawing pictures of Frankenstein's monster. Have students base the drawings on the description in the excerpt and not on pictures they have seen of Frankenstein's monster elsewhere.	

Note: For more tips, engagement strategies, and fluency options to include in this lesson, see pages 122–128.

Excerpt from *Frankenstein*

by Mary Shelley

It was on a dreary night of November that I beheld the accomplishment of my toils. With an anxiety that almost amounted to agony, I collected the instruments of life around me, that I might infuse a spark of being into the lifeless thing that lay at my feet. It was already one in the morning. The rain pattered dismally against the panes, and my candle was nearly burnt out, when, by the glimmer of the half-extinguished light, I saw the dull yellow eye of the creature open. It breathed hard, and a convulsive motion agitated its limbs.

How can I describe my emotions at this catastrophe, or how delineate the wretch whom with such infinite pains and care I had endeavored to form? His limbs were in proportion, and I had selected his features as beautiful. Beautiful! Great God! His yellow skin scarcely covered the work of muscles and arteries beneath. His hair was of a lustrous black, and owing; his teeth of a pearly whiteness; but these luxuriances only formed a more horrid contrast with his watery eyes, that seemed almost of the same color as the dun-white sockets in which they were set, his shriveled complexion and straight black lips.

His jaws opened, and he muttered some inarticulate sounds, while a grin wrinkled his cheeks. He might have spoken, but I did not hear. One hand was stretched out, seemingly to detain me, but I escaped and rushed downstairs. I took refuge in the courtyard belonging to the house which I inhabited, where I remained during the rest of the night, walking up and down in the greatest agitation, listening attentively, catching and fearing each sound as if it were to announce the approach of the demoniacal corpse to which I had so miserably given life.

Oh! No mortal could support the horror of that countenance. A mummy again endued with animation could not be so hideous as that wretch. I had gazed on him while unfinished; he was ugly then, but when those muscles and joints were rendered capable of motion, it became a thing such as even Dante could not have conceived.

I passed the night wretchedly. Sometimes my pulse beat so quickly and hardly that I felt the palpitation of every artery. At others, I nearly sank to the ground through languor and extreme weakness. Mingled with this horror, I felt the bitterness of disappointment. Dreams that had been my food and pleasant rest for so long a space were now become a hell to me; and the change was so rapid, the overthrow so complete!

Name: _____ Date: _____

Excerpt from *Frankenstein* Response

Directions: Reread the text on page 33 to answer each question.

1. What does it mean when the narrator (Dr. Frankenstein) says *he beheld the accomplishment of his toils*?

   Ⓐ He holds onto a prize.

   Ⓑ He looks at the result of his hard work.

   Ⓒ He works hard but fails anyway.

   Ⓓ He works until he is exhausted.

2. What part of the text indicates that Dr. Frankenstein wishes he had not brought the creature to life?

   _____
   _____
   _____

3. How does Dr. Frankenstein describe how he feels after the corpse comes to life? Does his experiment turn out the way he planned?

   _____
   _____
   _____
   _____
   _____

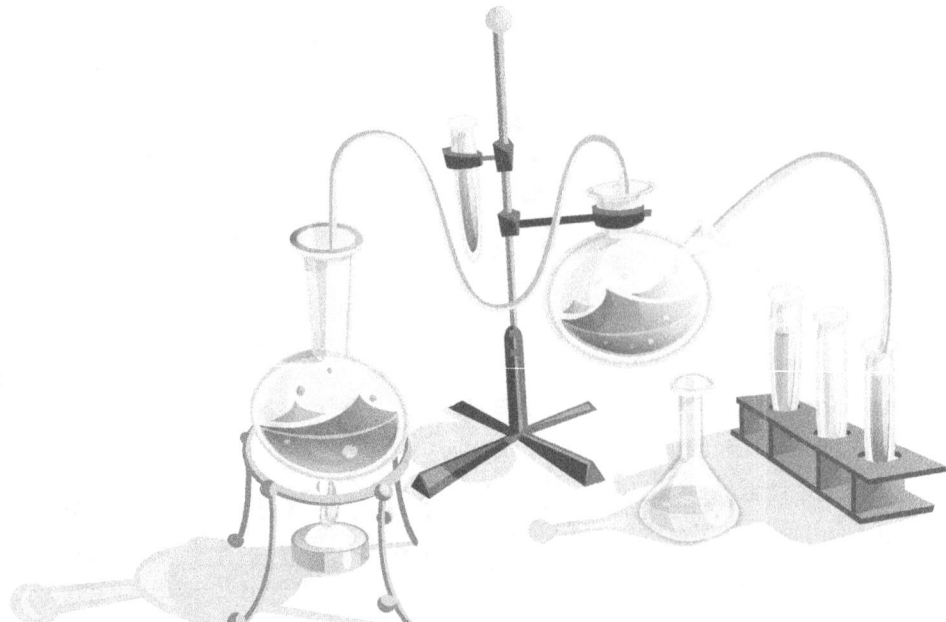

Name: _____ Date: _____

Let's Compare!
The Frankenstein Story

Directions: Reread both texts. Use information from both texts to complete the Venn diagram. What did you learn from the nonfiction text? What did you learn from the fiction text? What did you learn from both?

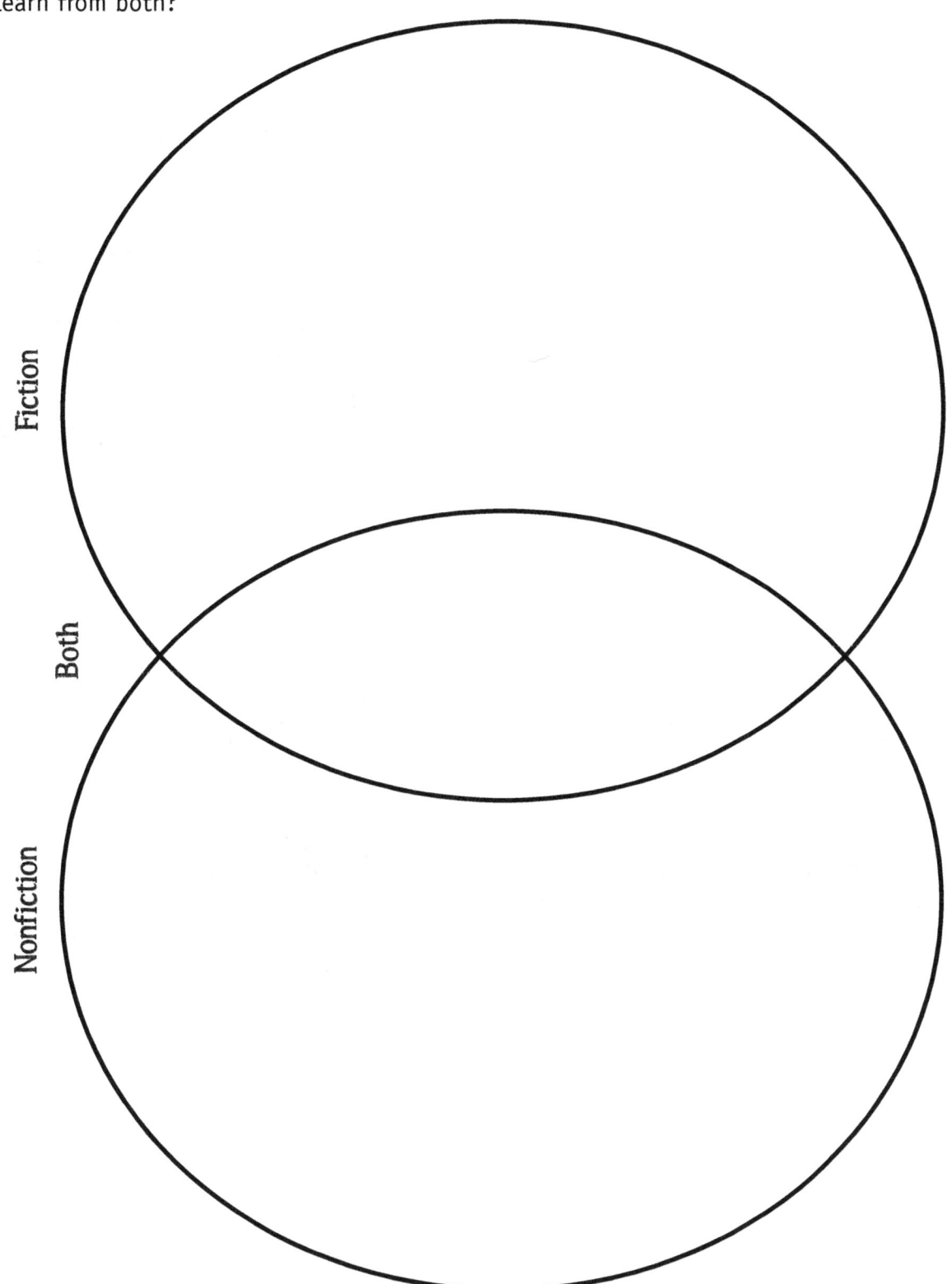

© Shell Education 51735—Close Reading with Paired Texts

Name: _____ Date: _____

Thinking About Monster Movies

Directions: Choose at least two of these activities to complete.

 ## Expanding Reading

Reread the excerpt from *Frankenstein*. Do a quick Internet search for Mary Shelley's inspiration for writing Frankenstein. Write a short report on why she wrote the story.

 ## Building Fluency

With a partner, practice reading the excerpt from *Frankenstein*. Take turns reading every other paragraph. Focus on the use of expression to communicate that the narrator (Dr. Frankenstein) is afraid. Perform your dramatic reading for another group of students.

 ## Exploring Words

Review the excerpt from *Frankenstein*. Create a list of words that the author uses to communicate fear. Put the words in order from least fearful to most fearful.

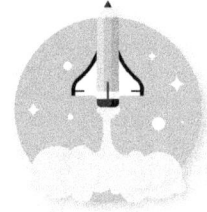 ## Crafting Writing

Imagine you are a television reporter telling a story about the history of monster movies. Write the script you would use for telling the story to viewers.

Unit 4 Overview
Geometry

Theme Summary

There are examples of geometry in the world all around us. In this lesson, students will read a nonfiction text about angles, triangles, and lines. They will also read a fiction text analyzing geometric figures from different perspectives.

Standards

- Determine a central idea of a text and analyze its development over the course of the text, including how it emerges and is shaped and refined by specific details; provide an objective summary of the text.
- Determine a theme or central idea of a text and how it is conveyed through particular details; provide a summary of the text distinct from personal opinions or judgments.
- Draw, construct, and describe geometrical figures, and describe the relationships between them.

Materials

- *Shapes in Geometry* (page 39)
- *"Shapes in Geometry" Response* (page 40)
- *Excerpt from* Flatland (page 42)
- *Excerpt from* Flatland *Response* (page 43)
- *Let's Compare! Living in Space and Flatland* (page 44)
- *Thinking About Geometry* (page 45)

Comparing the Texts

After students complete the lessons for each text, have them work in pairs to reread both texts and complete *Let's Compare! Living in Space and Flatland* (page 44). Finally, students can work to complete the *Thinking About Geometry* matrix (page 45). The matrix activities allow students to work on important literacy skills of reading, writing, vocabulary, and fluency. For further text analysis, compare these texts to "Pi" by Wislawa Szymborska.

Answer Key

"Shapes in Geometry" Response (page 40)

1. C. a vertex
2. The angles are connected, making it a closed shape. The sides and angles connected together probably make it strong.
3. Answers may include the following: the spaces between the spokes on a wheel, the shape of some tortilla chips, a slice of pizza, Egyptian pyramids, or a yield sign.

Excerpt from *Flatland* Response (page 43)

1. C. understand
2. In Flatland, everything is at eye level, so shapes can't be seen. If we can only see the side of a shape, it's just a line. Space is like the world we live in on Earth. Objects and people are three-dimensional.
3. It's all about perspective. When peering down at a penny, we can see the dimension. When we move our eyes to be level with the penny, we can only see one side, and it appears to be just a line.

Let's Compare! Living in Space and Flatland (page 44)

The first drawing should show identifiable furniture: couch, chair, table, etc. The second drawing should consist of lines of varying lengths with one line to represent each furniture item in the first drawing.

Nonfiction Text Teacher Notes
Shapes in Geometry

	Lesson Steps	Teacher Think Alouds
Ready, Set, Predict!	• Provide the text for students and display a larger version to use as a model. • Direct students to read the first few words of each paragraph. Have them share their predictions about the text in pairs.	"Even if I only look at the first few words of each paragraph, I can get an idea of what the text is about."
Go!	• Have students read the text independently, drawing stars beside each of the three geometry concepts discussed (*angles, triangles, lines*). • Read the text aloud, modeling fluent reading and emphasizing appropriate reading rate.	"I didn't think about angles relating to roller coasters, but if I visualize a roller coaster, I can picture the angles."
Reread to Clarify	• Have students reread the text, underlining challenging words or ideas in the text to clarify what they read. • Direct students to share their understanding of how geometry concepts relate to real-life situations with partners.	
Reread to Question	• Invite students to reread the text in pairs for the purpose of questioning. Direct each student to write two questions that can be answered from the text. Have students discuss their questions and answers. • Have students respond to the questions and prompts on page 40.	
Reread to Summarize and Respond	• Have students make T-charts with geometry concepts on one side and real-life applications on the other. • Instruct them to reread the text to summarize. • Students should share their summaries with partners.	

*__Note:__ For more tips, engagement strategies, and fluency options to include in this lesson, see pages 122–128.

Shapes in Geometry

Angles

All figures are made up of points. One example is a ray, which starts at a single point and then stretches forever in one direction. An angle is made up of two rays that intersect at a point, which is called the vertex.

Angles are critically important in the construction of roller coasters. Designers have to ensure that the angles are not too steep, because that might make the roller coaster too dangerous. However, the angles have to be steep enough to make for a thrilling ride.

Triangles

The world around us is made up of lines, angles, and shapes. Look around your classroom, how many triangles can you find? How many angles can you see on your desk? Try to count the lines that make up the front of the room. I bet there are almost too many to count!

A triangle is a closed shape. It is two-dimensional. It has three line segments for its sides. It is a three-sided polygon. The sides meet at three points. These points are called vertices. Each vertex forms an angle with two of the sides. The word *triangle* means "three angles." You can measure the three angles. You can add up the measures of those angles. They always add up to 180°.

Triangles can be used to build things. They are strong shapes. Some rooftops are shaped like triangles. So are some parts of ceilings and bridges.

Lines

There are many kinds of lines. Parallel lines will never cross. They will always be the same distance apart. When lines cross, they intersect at one point.

Lines, rays, and segments can intersect. When they do, angles are formed. You know that a right angle is 90°. When right angles are formed, the lines, rays, or segments that formed those angles are perpendicular.

Look at the room shown. There are many examples of both types of lines. The pictures, table, chair, and drawers are only a few. If the handrail was not parallel with the base of the posts, it could cause problems. If the stair steps were not parallel with each other and with the ground, then anyone using the steps would likely fall!

Name: _____ Date: _____

▢Shapes in Geometry▢ Response

Directions: Reread the text on page 39 to answer each question.

1. What is the point of a triangle called?

    Ⓐ an angle　　　　　　　　Ⓒ a vertex

    Ⓑ a ray　　　　　　　　　Ⓓ a closed shape

2. Why is a triangle considered to be a strong shape?

    _____
    _____
    _____

3. Where in your life do you encounter triangles?

    _____
    _____
    _____
    _____
    _____

Fiction Text Teacher Notes
Excerpt from *Flatland*

	Lesson Steps	Teacher Think Alouds
Ready, Set, Predict!	• Have students read the title and predict how the excerpt from *Flatland* might be related to the theme of geometry. • Provide students with the text and display a larger version for the class to see as you model.	
Go!	• Have students read the text independently. Direct them to underline any words or concepts they do not understand. • Read the text aloud as students follow along. Model the use of appropriate pausing when encountering commas and dashes.	"The second paragraph has two dashes used to insert a clause. When I read that sentence, I will pause briefly at each dash."
Reread to Clarify	• Have students reread the excerpt to clarify words and ideas. Students should underline words that they help them visualize Flatland. • Instruct them to meet with partners to discuss the parts of the text they underlined to determine meaning. Encourage students to discuss whether rereading or "reading on" was the most helpful strategy to unlock meaning.	
Reread to Question	• Tell students to reread the text for the purpose of questioning. Have them ask questions about the author's purpose for writing. • Have students meet in pairs to share their questions and discuss answers.	"What does the author want to communicate to us through the text?"
Reread to Summarize and Respond	• Have partners work together to summarize the excerpt using four sentences. • Then, challenge pairs to summarize the text using three sentences, then two, then one.	"Each time I shorten the summary, I have to think of the most important part of the text to keep."

*Note: For more tips, engagement strategies, and fluency options to include in this lesson, see pages 122–128.

Excerpt from *Flatland*

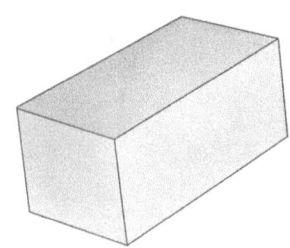

By Edwin A. Abbott

This story is about two different worlds called Flatland and Space.

I call our world Flatland, not because we call it so, but to make its nature clearer to you, my happy readers, who are privileged to live in Space.

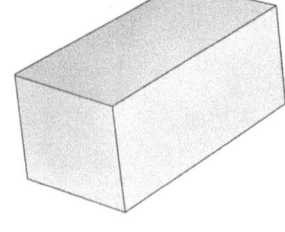

Imagine a vast sheet of paper on which straight Lines, Triangles, Squares, Pentagons, Hexagons, and other figures, instead of remaining fixed in their places, move freely about, on or in the surface, but without the power of rising above or sinking below it, very much like shadows—only hard with luminous edges—and you will then have a pretty correct notion of my country and countrymen. Alas, a few years ago, I should have said "my universe," but now my mind has been opened to higher views of things.

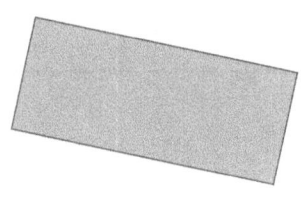

In such a country, you will perceive at once that it is impossible that there should be anything of what you call a "solid" kind, but I dare say you will suppose that we could at least distinguish by sight the Triangles, Squares, and other figures, moving about as I have described them. On the contrary, we could see nothing of the kind, not at least so as to distinguish one figure from another. Nothing is visible, nor could be visible, to us, except Straight Lines; and the necessity of this I will speedily demonstrate.

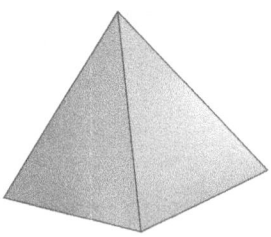

Place a penny on the middle of one of your tables in Space; and leaning over it, look down upon it. It will appear a circle.

But now, drawing back to the edge of the table, gradually lower your eye (thus bringing yourself more and more into the condition of the inhabitants of Flatland), and you will find the penny becoming more and more oval to your view, and at last when you have placed your eye exactly on the edge of the table (so that you are, as it were, actually a Flatlander), the penny will then have ceased to appear oval at all, and will have become, so far as you can see, a straight line.

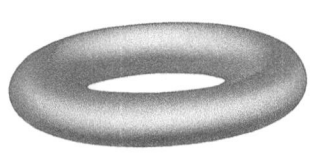

Name: _____ Date: _____

Excerpt from *Flatland* Response

Directions: Reread the text on page 42 to answer each question.

1. Which is a synonym for *perceive*?

   (A) perspective

   (B) distinguish

   (C) understand

   (D) dimension

2. How is Flatland different from space?

   _____
   _____
   _____

3. Explain the part of the text where a penny appears to be a straight line. Do you agree that the penny would appear as a straight line? Why or why not?

   _____
   _____
   _____
   _____

Name: _____ Date: _____

Let's Compare!
Living in Space and Flatland

Directions: Reread both texts. In the first box, draw a picture of a living room with various pieces of furniture as seen from the perspective of a person between 4 and 6 feet (1.22–1.83 meters) tall. In the second box, draw the same living room as it would be perceived in Flatland. Label your drawings.

Name: _____ Date: _____

Thinking About Geometry

Directions: Choose at least two of these activities to complete.

 ## Expanding Reading

Reread the excerpt from *Flatland*. Write a note telling how the narrator feels about living in Flatland. Use evidence from the text.

 ## Building Fluency

Read the excerpt from *Flatland* with a partner. The narrator explains a concept related to perspective. When explaining, we often speak a bit more slowly. Read the excerpt to a partner, and focus on slowing down your reading rate.

 ## Exploring Words

Review "Shapes in Geometry." What other words can you think of that use the root *tri* to indicate 3s?

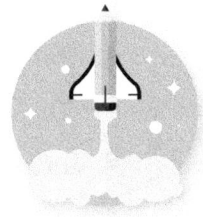 ## Crafting Writing

Write a paragraph or poem about how you use various geometric shapes in your everyday life. For example, tires are circles and are used to make cars move.

Unit 5 Overview
Fractals

Theme Summary

Fractals are nature's geometry. With this text pair, students will learn to take notice of the shapes and patterns in nature. They will read a nonfiction text explaining fractals and a poem about the scene after a snowstorm.

Answer Key

"Figuring Out Fractals" Response (page 49)

1. D. a person who is skilled in geometry
2. A. a shape the is self-similar and complex
3. The tree has miniature replicas of the whole tree. Each branch resembles the tree, and smaller branches on the branch resemble the tree. Fractals have self-similarity, and the structure of the branches is similar to the structure of the tree.
4. It means that the concept has not been around for very long.

"On Snow" Response (page 51)

1. B. trap
2. I can visualize the snow falling softly. I can also see the snowball someone squeezed together.
3. A snowflake is a series of repeated patterns, like a fractal.
4. Some of the adjectives the author uses to paint a picture are bright, light, heavy, dark, foulest.

Let's Compare! Shapes in Nature (page 53)

Students' letters should include information from the nonfiction text to explain fractals and examples from the poem to illustrate what they are. For example, a student might explain that fractals are patterns and shapes in the world around us.

Standards

- Determine a central idea of a text and how it is conveyed through particular details; provide a summary of the text distinct from personal opinions or judgments.
- Determine the meaning of words and phrases as they are used in a text.
- Understands that mathematics is the study of any pattern or relationship.
- Analyze patterns and relationships.

Materials

- *Figuring Out Fractals* (pages 48–49)
- *"Figuring Out Fractals" Response* (page 49)
- *"On Snow"* (page 51)
- *"On Snow" Response* (page 52)
- *Let's Compare! Shapes in Nature* (page 53)
- *Thinking About Fractals* (page 54)

Comparing the Texts

After students complete the lessons for each text, have them work in pairs to reread both texts and complete *Let's Compare! Shapes in Nature* (page 53). Finally, students can work to complete the *Thinking About Fractals* matrix (page 54). The matrix activities allow students to work on important literacy skills of reading, writing, vocabulary, and fluency.

Nonfiction Text Teacher Notes
Figuring Out Fractals

		Lesson Steps	Teacher Think Alouds
	Ready, Set, Predict!	• Provide the text for students and display a larger version to model during the lesson. • Have students pair up to read and discuss the title and headings. What do they predict the text will be about? Why did the author write this?	"*Fractal* sounds like *fraction*. How does that relate to geometry and nature?"
	Go!	• Have students read the text independently, underlining any words or concepts that teach them something they did not already know. • Read the text aloud, modeling fluent reading. Point out to students the importance of reading with accuracy.	
	Reread to Clarify	• Have students reread to clarify at least one word or one sentence that is confusing. • Have students revisit the new concepts they underlined to clarify their understanding. Then, have students share ways to clarify such as rereading, reading on, analyzing word parts, and visualizing.	"The term *ad infinitum* is new to me, but I can see from the spelling that it connects to the word *infinity*."
	Reread to Question	• Have students get into pairs. Then, have students reread the text to question. Instruct them to write questions in the margins related to fractals in nature. Have students work together, reading through the text again to find text evidence that answers their questions. • Have students respond to the questions and prompts on page 49.	
	Reread to Summarize and Respond	• Instruct students to reread the text to summarize. Have them identify the definition of fractals, a few examples of fractals in nature, and think of final statements. Instruct each student to write a favorite line on a strip of paper. Have students work in teams to share their chosen lines and then order them into group poems.	"Before I write my summary, I'll review the text again. I will circle the definition of fractals, underline some examples of fractals, and decide on a final sentence."

*****Note:** For more tips, engagement strategies, and fluency options to include in this lesson, see pages 122–128.

Figuring Out Fractals

By Theo Buchanan

Nature's Geometry

Nature is mysterious. With the seasonal changes in scenery come changes in geometry that often seem unexplainable. Looking at this photo of a tree, you can probably imagine roots extending into the soil below what is pictured. But what if I told you that this isn't really a tree because it's just a branch someone stuck into the snow? Isn't it easy to see how it could be both? That is because the structure of a branch is similar to that of a tree.

Branches make up trees, but they also look like smaller versions of trees. We call this *self-similarity*. In a self-similar pattern, pieces of the pattern are miniature replicas of the whole. And that means that within those replicas, there will be even smaller replicas. This replication either stops at a certain scale or continues *ad infinitum* (to infinity). Take a look at a small tree branch coming out from a larger branch and notice, again, the tree-like structure. In a large tree, you can see dozens, sometimes even hundreds of mini trees! This is an example of a fractal.

What's the Definition?

Fractals come in a huge variety of forms, but they are generally defined as shapes that exhibit self-similarity and high complexity. As you will see, these shapes appear in many different forms throughout nature.

Fractals Everywhere!

"Why is geometry often described as 'cold' and 'dry'? One reason lies in its inability to describe the shape of a cloud, a mountain, a coastline, or a tree. Clouds are not spheres, mountains are not cones, coastlines are not circles." —Mathematician and "fractalist" Benoit Mandelbrot

Fractal geometry is a mathematical infant. The term *fractal* has only existed since Mandelbrot, the "father of fractals," published his book, *The Fractal Geometry of Nature*, in 1982. This is amazing because for as long as humans have inhabited Earth, they have been surrounded by these patterns, and not in any small way either. As Mandelbrot points out, some of the largest features of our planet are fractals.

Fluffy Fractals!

A photo taken of a cloud formation up close will also show a remarkable level of scale invariance. This is because each individual "puff" is made up of smaller puffs. Clouds are good examples of why the term *fractal* doesn't need a strict definition. It's nearly always true that each puff has a somewhat unique shape, so clouds are really not *strictly* self-similar. But because all the shapes are so random, clouds are definitely scale invariant, making them fractals.

Figuring Out Fractals (cont.)

But Mom, I'm Drawing Fractals!

Benoit Mandelbrot himself said he made his famous discovery while having "mindless fun," and geometers around the world have enjoyed creating their own fractals from simple sets of rules. So get curious and get creative! Fractals are out in the world to be seen and are living in your mind, waiting to be created.

In comics, mountains are often shown as triangles. Even a photograph of a mountain will often appear to be roughly triangular, but this triangle is rough because it is made up of many smaller triangles. These smaller triangles are rough because they are also made up of smaller ones, and so on.

"Figuring Out Fractals" Response

Directions: Reread the text on pages 48–49 to answer each question.

1. What is the meaning of *geometer*? (Use context clues to help you.)

   Ⓐ a tool to measure geometric shapes   Ⓒ the study of geometry

   Ⓑ a unit of measure   Ⓓ a person who is skilled in geometry

2. What is a fractal?

   Ⓐ a shape that is self-similar and complex   Ⓒ a triangle made of other triangles

   Ⓑ a shape that does not repeat   Ⓓ puffs made of smaller puffs

3. How does the photograph of the tree branch help you to understand the concept of fractals?
   _____
   _____
   _____

4. What is meant by *fractal geometry is a mathematical infant*?
   _____
   _____
   _____

Fiction Text Teacher Notes
On Snow

	Lesson Steps	Teacher Think Alouds
Ready, Set, Predict!	• Provide students with the poem, and display a larger version for the class to see while you model. • Have students read the title and predict how the poem might relate to fractals. Students should share their predictions with partners.	
Go!	• Invite students to read the poem independently, underlining phrases they have difficulty visualizing. • Read the text aloud as students follow along. Demonstrate the use of repetition by reading the last line of the stanza twice.	"When I read the last line of the stanza twice, it places emphasis on that line."
Reread to Clarify	• Have students reread the poem to clarify what they are visualizing. Instruct them to circle portions of the text that help them to picture the shape of the snow. • Have students meet in pairs to discuss the text they circled and what it communicates about fractals.	"When I read the poem to clarify, my understanding of it increases when I visualize what the author describes."
Reread to Question	• Tell students to reread the text for the purpose of questioning. Have them share their questions with partners and find clues in the text to answer them. Provide sentence frames such as: Why did the author… I wonder about… How did the author…	
Reread to Summarize and Respond	• Instruct partners to work together to write what they think about the first snow of the season. Encourage partners to make drawings to illustrate the poem.	

***Note:** For more tips, engagement strategies, and fluency options to include in this lesson, see pages 122–128.

Name: _____ Date: _____

On Snow

By Jonathan Swift

A Riddle

From Heaven I fall, though from earth I begin.
No lady alive can show such a skin.
I'm bright as angel, and light as a feather,
But heavy and dark, when you squeeze me together.
Though candor and truth in my aspect I bear,
Yet many poor creatures I help to insnare.
Though so much of Heaven appears in my make,
The foulest impressions I easily take.
My parents and I produce one another,
The mother the daughter, the daughter the mother.

Name: _____ Date: _____

"On Snow" Response

Directions: Reread the text on page 51 to answer each question.

1. What does *insnare* mean?

   Ⓐ set free   Ⓒ to scare

   Ⓑ trap   Ⓓ eat

2. Describe the scene that you visualize while reading the text.
   _____
   _____
   _____

3. How is a snowflake a fractal?
   _____
   _____
   _____
   _____

4. List 5 descriptive words that help you visualize the image the author is painting with his words.
   _____
   _____

Name: _____　　　　Date: _____

Let's Compare!
Shapes in Nature

Directions: Reread both texts. Write a letter explaining what fractals are. Use examples of fractals from the poem.

Dear _____ ,
　　　　　(name)

_____
_____
_____
_____
_____
_____
_____
_____
_____
_____
_____
_____
_____
_____
_____
_____
_____
_____

　　　　　　　　　　　　　　　　　　　　　Sincerely,

　　　　　　　　　　　　　　　　　　　　　_____

Name: _____ Date: _____

Thinking About Fractals

Directions: Choose at least two of these activities to complete.

Expanding Reading

Reread "On Snow." Highlight a part of the text that conjures up a strong visual image. Write a note about it in the margin.

Building Fluency

Read "On Snow" with a partner. Think about the setting and the hushed tones of nature. Read in a way that emphasizes a calm, quiet mood. Read it a second time in a different tone of voice. Perform the poem, taking turns. Ask listeners to share what each version conveys.

Exploring Words

Fractals and fractions come from the same root. How are fractals and fractions alike or not alike? What other words, using the root *frac-*, can you think of?

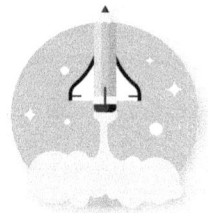
Crafting Writing

Choose two lines from "On Snow." Rewrite them using your own words, and draw an illustration that reflects the scene.

Unit 6 Overview
Cryptography

Theme Summary

Cryptography is the practice of creating secret messages to protect information. In this lesson, students will read a nonfiction text about cryptography and ciphers. They will also read a fiction text about solving a mysterious riddle. Many ciphers are created using mathematical patterns. You must know the function used to decrypt the cipher.

Standards

- Determine the meaning of words and phrases as they are used in a text, including figurative and connotative meanings; analyze the impact of a specific word choice on meaning and tone.
- Cite textual evidence to support analysis of what the text says explicitly as well as inferences drawn from the text.
- Generalizes from a pattern of observations made in particular cases, makes conjectures, and provides supporting arguments for these conjectures.
- Understands that mathematics is the study of any pattern or relationship.

Materials

- *Mysterious Cryptography* (pages 57–58)
- *"Mysterious Cryptography" Response* (page 58)
- *Excerpt from* The Riddle of the Sphinx (pages 60–61)
- *Excerpt from* The Riddle of the Sphinx *Response* (page 61)
- *Let's Compare! Ciphers vs. Riddles* (page 62)
- *Thinking About Cryptography* (page 63)

Comparing the Texts

After students complete the lessons for each text, have them work in pairs to reread both texts and complete *Let's Compare! Ciphers vs. Riddles* (page 62). Finally, students can work to complete the *Thinking About Cryptography* matrix (page 63). The matrix activities allow students to work on important literacy skills of reading, writing, vocabulary, and fluency.

Answer Key

"Mysterious Cryptography" Response (page 58)

1. D. all of the above
2. Cipher makers use mathematical patterns to jumble up their messages.
3. Coded messages might be used in war to tell troops of a plan to attack the enemy, or to keep personal information safe from hackers.

Excerpt from *The Riddle of the Sphinx* Response (page 61)

1. A. Oedipus feels his blood boil within him.
2. The Sphinx is planning to eat him. She refers to him as a *dainty morsel* and says he has *fresh, young limbs*.
3. He is educated, had spoken with wise men, and learned great secrets.

Let's Compare! Ciphers vs. Riddles (page 62)

- Cipher: secret message, uses mathematics and patterns, letters of the text are jumbled up and replaced with different letters, numbers, and symbols.
- Riddle: a question that is meant to be confusing, a kind of puzzle that must be solved.
- Both: use mathematics and patterns, must be solved, messages are a mystery.

Nonfiction Text Teacher Notes

Mysterious Cryptography

	Lesson Steps	Teacher Think Alouds
Ready, Set, Predict!	• Provide the text for students, and display a larger version for the class to see while you model. • Have students review the headings and predict what cryptography is and what they will learn about it. Have them share their thoughts in pairs.	"By reading the headings "Ciphers," "Cipher Machines," and "Into the Future," I can get an idea of what cryptography means and what I may learn about it. The root *graph* is related to writing, so this provides a clue."
Go!	• Have students read the text independently, circling words that are new to them or ones that are unique to the topic. • Read the text aloud, modeling fluent reading. As you read, demonstrate how to pause briefly when encountering commas.	
Reread to Clarify	• Have students reread the text to clarify words and ideas that are challenging or unique to the topic. • Direct students to meet in pairs to discuss words and strategies for determining the meanings of unfamiliar words and complex ideas.	
Reread to Question	• Have students reread the text in pairs for the purpose of questioning. Have each student ask a question beginning with *what* or *why*. • Have students respond to the questions and prompts on page 58.	"Three simple questions I could ask are, 'What is cryptography?' 'Why is cryptography important?' and 'How is it used?' As I read, I may consider more complex questions, such as 'How does cryptography compare to other ways of coding messages?' I'll try to think of more complex questions."
Reread to Summarize and Respond	• Instruct students to reread the text to summarize. Have them summarize what cryptography is and why it is used. Have them work in teams to act out the content in each section.	

*Note: For more tips, engagement strategies, and fluency options to include in this lesson, see pages 122–128.

56   51735—*Close Reading with Paired Texts*   © Shell Education

Mysterious Cryptography

By Rane Anderson

Imagine you're standing in an old, quiet graveyard in England. Every dreary headstone looks the same—except one. The headstone displays the usual name and date but also has several strange, unreadable symbols carved into the stone. What could they mean?

This true-life mystery from the nineteenth century stumped everyone who saw the odd progression of symbols. It caught the attention of reporters and authors, mystifying many. Some people said the symbols were Greek letters. Others thought they might be Hebrew letters. But the truth was that only a select group, the Freemasons, could understand the inscription.

In the eighteenth century, Freemasons used the same symbols to create cryptographs, or coded messages. Afraid of persecution for their beliefs, they disguised their potentially dangerous ideas and records in secret ciphers. By using numbers, letters, and symbols to make ciphers, they sent and received messages nobody else could understand.

Ciphers

Unlike codes, where each word or message is replaced with another word or symbol, mathematics and patterns play large roles in creating ciphers. In a cipher, every letter in a message is replaced. Cipher makers use special procedures to jumble up plaintext—the letters that make up a correspondence prior to encryption—with different letters, words, numbers, or symbols. These procedures vary in difficulty. Can you identify the procedure used to create this simple cipher?

> rekaerbedoc emosewa na ma i

You might have figured out that the plaintext reads, *I am an awesome codebreaker*. The procedure for this cipher included only one step: to write the message backwards.

A two-step procedure might look a little different. Can you figure out the difference?

> reka erbe docemo sew ana mai

In the second step of this cipher, the letters are separated at different intervals.

These are simple examples, but ciphers today rely on complex mathematics to decrypt and encrypt—to convert into a scrambled message.

Name: _____ Date: _____

Mysterious Cryptography (cont.)

Cipher Machines

Computers now help us create sophisticated ciphers, but long ago, people had to rely on their wits alone to devise new and clever methods of making cryptographs. Eventually, this led to the invention of simple devices that could generate complicated ciphers.

Into the Future

Cryptography is a mighty tool that can be used for good and for bad. The techniques to encode messages have evolved over time, but the goals remain the same. Cryptographers strive to protect top-secret information from interception. They also need to intercept messages to prevent tragedies, such as wars and terrorism.

For the average person, cryptography remains behind the scenes. It's intertwined in the everyday tasks people complete online, on cell phones, and on other devices. But it is always there, thanks to the scholars and codebreakers who worked through the centuries to turn cryptography into what it is today.

▫Mysterious Cryptography▫ Response

Directions: Reread the text on pages 57–58 to answer each question.

1. Which of the following is a synonym for *cryptography*?

    Ⓐ coded message   Ⓒ secret message

    Ⓑ cipher   Ⓓ all of the above

2. How do cipher makers use mathematics and patterns to create their ciphers?
    _____
    _____
    _____

3. How could cryptography be used for both good and bad purposes?
    _____
    _____
    _____
    _____

Fiction Text Teacher Notes

Excerpt from *The Riddle of the Sphinx*

		Lesson Steps	Teacher Think Alouds
	Ready, Set, Predict!	• Provide students with the text, and display a larger version so you can model how to write on it. • Have students share what they know about solving a problem. Then, have them read the title. Encourage them to predict how a riddle might relate to solving a problem.	
	Go!	• Have students read the text independently. Direct them to underline challenging or interesting words and discuss them in pairs. • Read the text aloud as students follow along. Model the use of expression in the dialogue.	"I'm going to think about how the evil sphinx might sound and change my expression when I read her words."
	Reread to Clarify	• Ask students to reread the excerpt to clarify. Instruct them to use evidence from the text to better understand the challenging words they identified. • Have students meet in pairs to discuss the text they underlined.	
	Reread to Question	• Tell students to reread the text for the purpose of questioning. Have each student write a question on an index card. Then, have students meet in groups of three to four. Mix up the cards, and distribute them to group members. Each student should read the question on his or her card and answer it. Encourage the group to add their thoughts and discuss each question.	"When I answer questions, it is helpful to find specific evidence that points to the answer. For example, if I ask whether the Sphinx is a beast or a woman, I find in the beginning of the story that she used to be a woman and now she is a beast."
	Reread to Summarize and Respond	• Have partners work together to summarize the excerpt in one paragraph of four or five sentences. Then, have them create drawings to illustrate their summaries.	

*****Note:** For more tips, engagement strategies, and fluency options to include in this lesson, see pages 122–128.

Excerpt from *The Riddle of the Sphinx*

By Elsie Finnimore Buckley

In The Riddle of the Sphinx, *Oedipus (a king in Greek mythology) faces the sphinx to answer a riddle. If he tries to avoid her, she will kill the villagers. If he answers incorrectly, he will die. If he answers correctly, the Sphinx will leave them alone forever.*

"Oh, lady, I am come to hear thy famous riddle and answer it or die."

"Foolhardy manling, a dainty morsel the gods have sent this day, with thy fair young face and fresh young limbs."

And she licked her cruel lips.

Then Oedipus felt his blood boil within him, and he wished to slay her then and there; for she who had been the fairest of women was now the foulest of beasts, and he saw that by her cruelty and lust she had killed the woman's soul within her, and the soul of a beast had taken its place.

"Come, tell me thy famous riddle, foul Fury that thou art, that I may answer it and rid the land of this curse."

"At dawn it creeps on four legs; at noon it strides on two; at sunset and evening it totters on three. What is this thing, never the same, yet not many, but one?"

So she chanted slowly, and her eyes gleamed cruel and cold.

Then thought Oedipus within himself,

"Now or never must my learning and wit stand me in good stead, or in vain have I talked with the wisest of men and learnt the secrets of Phoenicia and Egypt."

Excerpt from *The Riddle of the Sphinx* (cont.)

And the gods who had given him understanding sent light into his heart, and boldly he answered, "What can this creature be but man, O Sphinx? For, a helpless babe at the dawn of life, he crawls on his hands and feet; at noontide he walks erect in the strength of his manhood; and at evening he supports his tottering limbs with a staff, the prop and stay of old age. Have I not answered aright and guessed thy famous riddle?"

Then with a loud cry of despair, and answering him never a word, the great beast sprang up from her seat on the rock and hurled herself over the precipice into the yawning gulf beneath. Far away across the plain, the people heard her cry, and they saw the flash of the sun on her brazen wings like a gleam of lightning in the summer sky. Thereupon, they sent up a great shout of joy to heaven and poured out from every gate into the open plain, and some raised Oedipus upon their shoulders and, with shouts and songs of triumph, bore him to the city. Then and there, they made him king with one accord, for the old king had left no son behind him, and who more fitted to rule over them than the slayer of the Sphinx and the saviour of their city?

Excerpt from *The Riddle of the Sphinx* Response

Directions: Reread the text on pages 60–61 to answer each question.

1. Which of the following is an example of figurative language that shows Oedipus is angry?

   A) Oedipus feels his blood boil within him.

   B) He wishes to slay her then and there.

   C) The soul of a beast has taken its place.

   D) At dawn it creeps on four legs.

2. What does the Sphinx plan to do with Oedipus if he cannot solve the riddle? Provide evidence from the text.

   _____
   _____
   _____

3. How did Oedipus solve the riddle?

   _____
   _____
   _____
   _____

Name:_____ Date:_____

Let's Compare!
Ciphers vs. Riddles

Directions: Reread both texts. Describe the difference between ciphers and riddles. Use information from the texts to help you. Be sure to include information about how ciphers and riddles use mathematics.

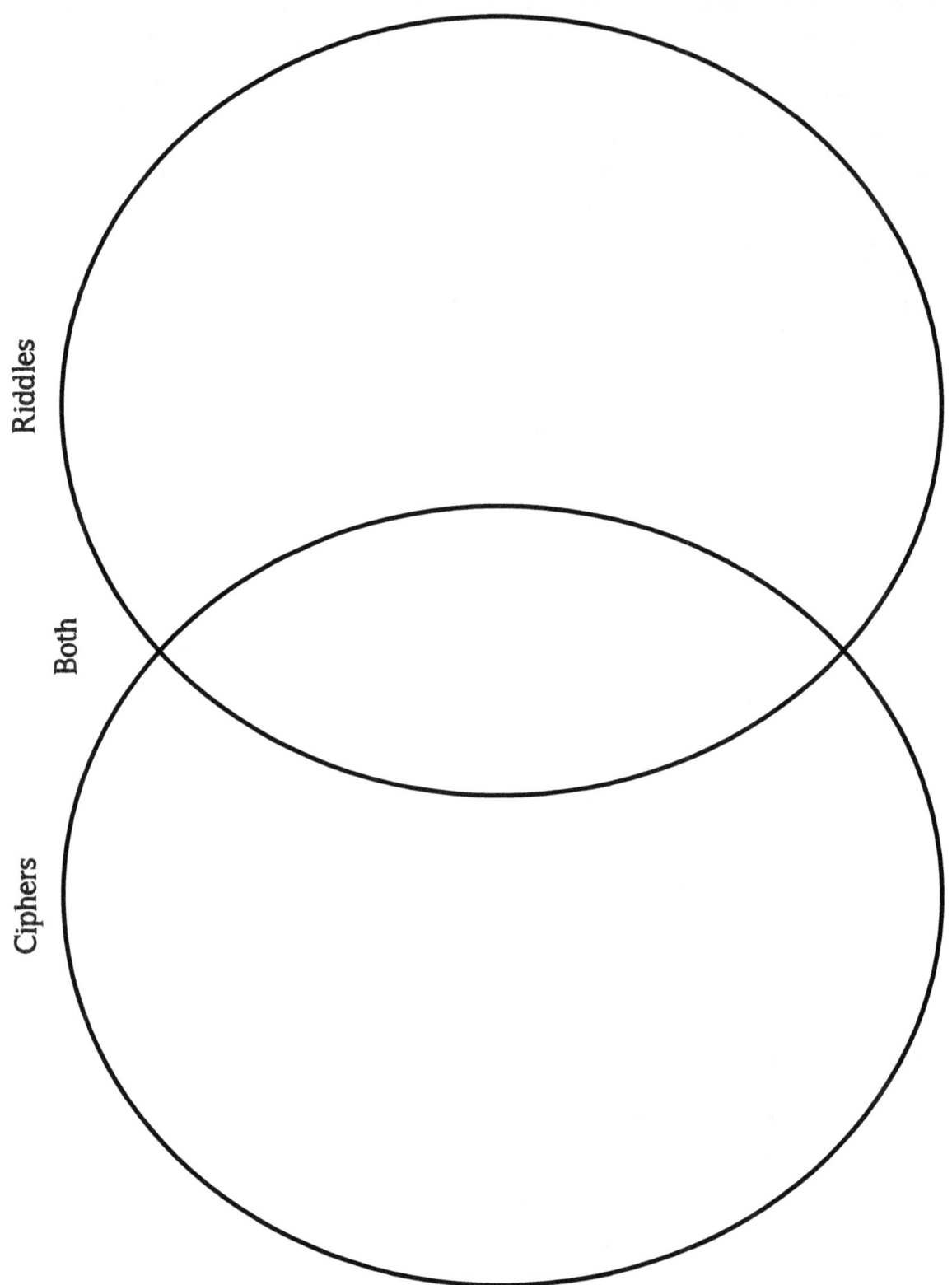

Name:_____ Date:_____

Thinking About Cryptography

Directions: Choose at least two of these activities to complete.

 ## Expanding Reading

Reread "Mysterious Cryptography." In the margin, write a coded message using the second cipher example. Then research Enigma from World War II and write a paragraph about how countries used coded messages during the war.

 ## Building Fluency

Read the excerpt from *The Riddle of the Sphinx* in a group of three. Identify one person to read the part of the Sphinx, one to read the part of Oedipus, and one to be the narrator. Focus on reading dialogue with appropriate expression.

 ## Exploring Words

Review "Mysterious Cryptography." Make a list of other words that contain the root word *graph*. What meaning do they have in common?

Examples:

- graphic novel
- autograph
- paragraph
- telegraph
- mimeograph
- dysgraphia

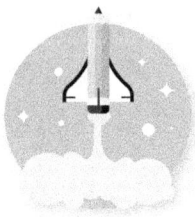 ## Crafting Writing

Create a cipher message. Exchange ciphers with another student, and try to decode the secret message. Share with your partner the cipher used to create the message. Use a different cipher from the example.

Example:

Uijt jt b dpefe nfttbhf.
This is a coded message.
Cipher: move the letter up one in the alphabet

© Shell Education 51735—Close Reading with Paired Texts

Unit 7 Overview
Engineering and Technology

Theme Summary

Engineering and technology are exciting fields. The creative, innovative possibilities are endless. In this lesson, students will read a nonfiction text about careers in engineering and technology. They will also read a fiction text describing a technology competition.

Answer Key

"STEM Careers: Enhancing Engineering" Response (page 67)

1. A. solving problems

2. Engineers have to build prototypes and then test them. If they don't work, they have to fix the problems or start again with new ideas.

3. Engineering and technology are related because they support each other. Engineering advances technology, and technology helps engineers create new products.

"STEM: The Battle Between 2-D and 3-D" Response (page 70)

1. B. He does not want to focus on it.

2. The text says Posie pops her gum. It also says her stomach does flip-flops, meaning she is nervous. These indicate that she is probably young. The text refers to Zak as a *gray-haired stranger*, so he is probably much older than Posie.

3. He has rooms filled with all different games. There are board games, hand-held games, and arcade games. He also does not ask Zak and Posie to make the same kind of games. He wants both 2-D and 3-D games.

Let's Compare! Careers in Technology and Engineering (page 71)

Responses will vary. Example answer:

What do you want to study in college? / I don't know yet. I want to make things better for people./Like what?/ I think I might want to go into engineering. / That sounds like fun./Yes!/ Maybe I'll do the same thing when I get to college!

Standards

⇒ Determine a central idea of a text and analyze its development over the course of the text, including how it emerges and is shaped and refined by specific details; provide an objective summary of the text.

⇒ Determine a theme or central idea of a text and how it is conveyed through particular details; provide a summary of the text distinct from personal opinions or judgments.

Materials

⇒ *STEM Careers: Enhancing Engineering* (pages 66–67)
⇒ *"STEM Careers: Enhancing Engineering" Response* (page 67)
⇒ *STEM: The Battle Between 2-D and 3-D* (pages 69–70)
⇒ *"STEM: The Battle Between 2-D and 3-D" Response* (page 70)
⇒ *Let's Compare! Careers in Technology and Engineering* (page 71)
⇒ *Thinking About Engineering and Technology* (page 72)

Comparing the Texts

After students complete the lessons for each text, have them work in pairs to reread both texts and complete *Let's Compare! Careers in Technology and Engineering* (page 71). Finally, students can work to complete the *Thinking About Engineering and Technology* matrix (page 72). The matrix activities allow students to work on important literacy skills of reading, writing, vocabulary, and fluency.

Nonfiction Text Teacher Notes
STEM Careers: Enhancing Engineering

	Lesson Steps	Teacher Think Alouds
Ready, Set, Predict!	• Ask students what they know about science, technology, engineering, and mathematics. Share with students that STEM comes from the words science, technology, engineering, and mathematics. • Ask students to preview the title, headings, and photograph. Then, have students share briefly what they think they will learn from the article.	
Go!	• Provide the text for students, and display a larger version for the class to see while you model. • Have students read the text independently, underlining three interesting words. • Read the text aloud, modeling fluent reading. As you read, demonstrate how to accent the italicized words for emphasis.	"The words *exactly* in the first paragraph and *doing* in the second paragraph are italicized. I'm going to read those words a little more slowly and with emphasis to draw attention to them."
Reread to Clarify	• Invite students to reread the text to make sure they understand each section of text. • Have students circle challenging concepts using colored makers or pencils. Encourage them to share and clarify with partners.	
Reread to Question	• Have students reread the text in pairs for the purpose of asking questions. Direct students to write their questions in the margin of the text. Questions should be crafted around information students find interesting. • Have students respond to the questions and prompts on page 67.	"I'm curious about the table from IKEA. Will I have to set out all the ingredients for it to tell me what I could cook with them?"
Reread to Summarize and Respond	• Instruct students to reread the text to summarize. Have students summarize possible uses of engineering and technology and draw stars next to examples of how these fields advance our everyday lives.	

*****Note:** For more tips, engagement strategies, and fluency options to include in this lesson, see pages 122–128.

STEM Careers: Enhancing Engineering

By Wendy Conklin

Imagine you owned a robot that could sense a human's mood and emotions. What if someday you lived on the moon—or better yet, Mars? Or if your favorite pet dies, you have it cloned so that you can have another pet *exactly* like it. If any of this intrigues you, you might want to consider becoming an engineer.

Engineering is the field of technology where people come up with new ideas, build them, and then test their ideas. While an engineer is not strictly a scientist, engineering has a lot to do with science. A scientist observes things and has theoretical ideas. Engineers build machines, structures such as bridges or roads, and systems found in video games and smart phones. Engineering is applying science to solve problems in our everyday lives. It's *doing* science, but engineering also involves math, design, psychology, and creativity.

Engineers design and build things such as driveways, computer software, and flying suits. But, to say that someone is an engineer doesn't give us a clear idea of what he or she does beyond designing and building. The designing and building process involves steps and takes time.

Engineers affect our everyday lives. For example, think about the features on a smart phone and how these features improve our lives. Engineers came up with these ideas. They built prototypes based on their ideas, and then they tested these ideas to see if they worked. Many times, engineers have to "go back to the drawing board" by changing their ideas or completely starting over. It becomes a trial-and-error process.

Technology and Engineering Go Hand in Hand

Some engineers work on solutions for the future. They know that the technology does not exist yet, but that doesn't stop them from inventing new ideas for products.

Think about the popular store IKEA. The company wants to design a table for the future that can serve many functions. Using a camera mounted above the table, the table would be able to recognize the types of foods placed on its surface. The camera would then project onto the table various recipes and cooking tips for using that food. To ensure accurate measurements, the table could weigh each ingredient. It would know how to cook the food appropriately, such as boiling or frying, and could even keep a coffee cup warm. Cooks would be able to browse recipes and record their own cooking sessions at this table.

Name: _____ Date: _____

STEM Careers: Enhancing Engineering (cont.)

To create this table, engineers have to develop brand-new technologies that don't exist today. This new table will affect the way people live in the future. It will affect future kitchen designs, and it will impact the types of foods we cook. The engineers are not only designing something new and interesting, they are changing how we live.

Engineering the Future

So, does technology advance engineers? Or do engineers advance technology? Perhaps engineering and technology help to advance each other. It is difficult to separate the two. It takes engineering to develop technology. Technology has to be there for engineers to use. So, the next time you pick up a phone, ride in a car, or turn on the lights, stop to reflect. Think about the technology, and consider all the work engineers do to make these things possible.

"STEM Careers: Enhancing Engineering" Response

Directions: Reread the text on pages 66–67 to answer each question.

1. What is the main point of engineering?

    Ⓐ solving problems   Ⓒ curing diseases

    Ⓑ making computer games   Ⓓ making trains run

2. Why does the designing and building process in engineering take time?
    _____
    _____
    _____

3. How are engineering and technology related?
    _____
    _____
    _____

Fiction Text Teacher Notes
STEM: The Battle Between 2-D and 3-D

	Lesson Steps	Teacher Think Alouds
Ready, Set, Predict!	• Have students read the title and predict how 2-D and 3-D relate to STEM. Explain the difference between two-dimensional games and three-dimensional games. Ask them to discuss their predictions in pairs. • Provide students with the text, and project a larger version for the class to see.	
Go!	• Have students read the text independently. Direct them to underline challenging words and discuss them in pairs. • Read the text aloud as students follow along. Model the use of expression and phrasing. • After reading, share with students how you used expression to enhance their understanding of the text.	"I'm going to pay attention to words I might not understand. For example, I'll underline *underground amphitheater* because I'm not sure what that is."
Reread to Clarify	• Have students reread the excerpt, circling any words or parts of the text that are confusing to clarify. Instruct them to circle parts of the text that are confusing. • Have students meet in pairs to discuss the text they circled and discuss ways to figure them out, such as rereading or visualizing.	
Reread to Question	• Tell students to reread the text for the purpose of questioning. Direct them to ask questions about the 2-D and 3-D games Zak and Posie might make. • Have students meet in pairs to discuss questions and answers using textual evidence.	"Does Zak have a chance at winning if he makes 2-D games?" Why, or why not?
Reread to Summarize and Respond	• Have partners work together to summarize the excerpt in one paragraph of four or five sentences along with an illustration. Invite students to share with other student pairs.	

*Note: For more tips, engagement strategies, and fluency options to include in this lesson, see pages 122–128.

68   51735—Close Reading with Paired Texts   © Shell Education

STEM: The Battle Between 2-D and 3-D

By Georgia Beth

Posie pops her gum loudly. "Any idea what we're doing here?" she asks the gray-haired stranger standing next to her.

It has been a weird morning, but something tells her that the unexpected late-night message is just the beginning. Before Zak can answer, billionaire Vikram Patel appears at the gates. "Posie! Zak! Come in! Thank you for accepting my mysterious invitation."

"It's not every day that I get a personal summons from the owner of Phenomtech," Posie replies.

"I couldn't resist meeting the man who created *Org It*," Zak agrees.

Vikram waves the compliment away and ushers his guests into a large marble hallway. The space is elegant but sterile. "You may know me as the face of Phenomtech, but my passion is gaming."

He leads them deep into his mansion, revealing room after room filled with games. One room is dedicated to classic board games, and another room has arcade games from Tokyo. There are libraries of handheld games and other rooms with velvet-lined tables for playing. Posie nearly swallows her gum.

Vikram leads them down a long stairway to an underground amphitheater, where a small crowd of tech execs and gamers looks on. Zak and Posie take their places on the raised area at the center of the stage.

Then Vikram says, "Many of you know that I want to hire a new game designer—someone who can make Phenomtech the most popular gaming platform in the entire world. I think that this competition is the best way to interview Zak and Posie."

Interview? Posie's stomach starts doing flip-flops.

"Zak will create 2-D videogames, and Posie will work in 3-D virtual reality. There will be four rounds of competition, each focusing on a different shape. Whoever creates the best games will become the new Chief Designer at Phenomtech."

Visions of *Pacman* and *Sonic the Hedgehog* flash in Zak's head because his old favorites always come to mind whenever it is time to design a new game.

Name:_____ Date:_____

STEM: The Battle Between 2-D and 3-D (cont.)

Posie begins chewing her gum in slow motion, but her mind is moving at lightning speed. She silently vows to create something no one has ever imagined before.

"Do you accept this challenge?" Vikram asks Zak.

"I do."

"Do you accept this challenge?" Vikram asks Posie.

"I do."

"Then let the games begin!" he declares to the audience.

▫STEM: The Battle Between 2-D and 3-D▫ Response

Directions: Reread the text on pages 69–70 to answer each question.

1. What does it mean that Patel *waves the compliment away*?

    Ⓐ He is embarrassed by it.   Ⓒ The compliment upsets him.

    Ⓑ He does not want to focus on it.   Ⓓ He is shy.

2. What can you determine about the ages of Posie and Zak? Use text evidence to support your response.
    _____
    _____
    _____

3. How can you tell that Vikram Patel is a fan of all kinds of games?
    _____
    _____
    _____
    _____
    _____

Name: _____ Date: _____

Let's Compare!
Careers in Technology and Engineering

Directions: Reread both texts. Use information from both texts to help you write a text exchange between yourself and a younger sibling or student. These texts should be about possible careers in technology and engineering. The texts should be in speech bubbles much like you would see on a mobile phone.

Name: _____   Date: _____

Thinking About Engineering and Technology

Directions: Choose at least two of these activities to complete.

Expanding Reading

Reread "STEM Careers: Enhancing Engineering." Write a note in the margin with an idea for an innovative piece of furniture you could invent.

Building Fluency

Read "STEM: The Battle Between 2-D and 3-D" in groups of three. Think about the differences between Posie, Zak, and Patel and how they speak. Rewrite the text as a script. Recite the script, with each person playing a different character.

Exploring Words

Review "STEM Careers: Enhancing Engineering." Create a list of words you don't typically use in everyday language. Choose three of the words, and use them in a conversation with a partner.

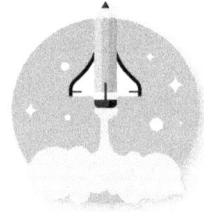

Crafting Writing

Imagine that Posie has the opportunity to interview Patel and Zak about their experience with technology and gaming. Write a newspaper article about their experience. If possible, post this article online.

Unit 8 Overview
Radiation

Theme Summary

Radiation is a dangerous energy that, when used properly, offers much to the world. In these paired texts, students will read about Marie Curie and her work as a scientist. They will also read a poem that expresses how Curie's work affected a family.

Standards

- Analyze in detail how a key individual, event or idea is introduced, illustrated, and elaborated in a text (e.g., through examples or anecdotes).
- Determine a theme or central idea of a text and how it is conveyed through particular details; provide a summary of the text distinct from personal opinions or judgments.
- Understands major discoveries in science and medicine in the first half of the 20th century (e.g., those made by Curie, Einstein, Freud) and how they affected the quality of life and traditional views of nature, the cosmos, and the psyche.

Materials

- *Marie Curie* (page 75)
- "Marie Curie" Response (page 76)
- *A Moment of Radiation* (page 78)
- "A Moment of Radiation" Response (page 79)
- *Let's Compare! Helpful and Harmful* (page 80)
- *Thinking About Radiation* (page 81)

Comparing the Texts

After students complete the lessons for each text, have them work in pairs to reread both texts and complete *Let's Compare! Helpful and Harmful* (page 80). Finally, students can work to complete the *Thinking About Radiation* matrix (page 81). The matrix activities allow students to work on important literacy skills of reading, writing, vocabulary, and fluency.

Answer Key

"Marie Curie" Response (page 76)

1. A. energy
2. We use radiation today to treat cancer, kill bacteria in food, and to determine the ages of fossils.
3. Working with radiation is dangerous and can make people sick. Curie's study of radiation eventually made her sick, and she died.
4. Curie discovered how to use radiation to treat cancer. She discovered that radiation could keep food from spoiling, detect smoke, and contribute to the study of dinosaur bones.

"A Moment of Radiation" Response (page 79)

1. C. Curie's work ended up killing her.
2. In Curie's time, it was not common for women to be scientists. People may have thought she was not capable enough.
3. The author is mostly concerned with the health of her mother and how Curie's work is saving her life.

Let's Compare! Helpful and Harmful (page 80)

- Helpful: used to treat cancer, used in smoke detectors, used to study dinosaur bones, kills organisms that spoil food, can detect weaknesses in bridges
- Harmful: exposure can cause cancer, can weaken eyesight, can burn skin, used to make atomic bombs

Nonfiction Text Teacher Notes
Marie Curie

	Lesson Steps	Teacher Think Alouds
Ready, Set, Predict!	• Provide the text for students, and project a larger version for the class to see. • Invite students to pair up to discuss the title and headings. Ask students to predict the ways she was an important scientist, how she discovered radium, and what happened in her final years.	
Go!	• Ask students to read the text independently, underlining scientific concepts that are new to them. • Read the text aloud, modeling fluent reading. Pause briefly before reading italicized words for emphasis.	"There are two italicized words in the text. I want to emphasize these when I read them aloud, so I will briefly pause before reading them."
Reread to Clarify	• Have students reread the text, underlining any parts or words that are confusing. • Have students revisit the new concepts they underlined to clarify their understanding. Then, have students share their thoughts in teams about the new concepts.	"I've heard of *radiation* being used to cure cancer, but I didn't realize how dangerous it was."
Reread to Question	• Have students work in pairs. Then, ask students to reread the text to question. Instruct them to write questions about radium, radiation, or the uses of radiation. Have students work together, reading through the text again to find text evidence that answers their questions. • Have students respond to the questions and prompts on page 76.	
Reread to Summarize and Respond	• Instruct students to reread the text to analyze how the author introduces Curie and elaborates on her accomplishments with examples. Draw stars beside each. Direct them to write summaries based on their analyses.	

*****Note:** For more tips, engagement strategies, and fluency options to include in this lesson, see pages 122–128.

Marie Curie

By Elizabeth Cregan and Dona Herwick Rice

Marie Curie is one of the most brilliant, important, and revolutionary scientists the world has ever known. She transformed the way people look at the world of energy and the resources available to us. But in doing so, she paid the ultimate price. She worked daily with radioactive materials, long before anyone knew their dangers. She took detailed notes of her observations and experiments, as a good scientist does. Little did she know, her painstaking work was slowly killing her.

An Important Scientist

Curie spent her life studying energy called *radiation*. In fact, she invented the word *radioactive* to describe this energy. Her investigations and experiments helped other scientists understand how atoms work. Curie also learned many things that became instrumental in finding new ways to treat cancer.

Discovering Radium

Curie suspected that the energy from uranium had to do with its atoms. Atoms are the basic building blocks that make up everything in the universe. Curie and her husband tested other elements to see if they generated radiation. This work led them to discover an element, which they named *radium*.

During this time, both scientists found themselves tired and losing weight. Their fingers were numb and burned. Perhaps they didn't realize that these symptoms were a result of handling radium. Some experts think the Curies knew radium would make them sick, but they ignored the dangers to continue their work.

The Final Years

Curie grew weaker and weaker from radiation sickness. Her eyesight was threatened, and finally, she became ill with cancer. In 1934, Curie died of the disease. The world mourned the loss of this great scientist.

But Curie had left a remarkable legacy. Her work led to many important findings, including the use of radiation to treat cancer, kill organisms that spoil food, find weaknesses in bridges, find smoke in homes, and even determine the age of dinosaur bones.

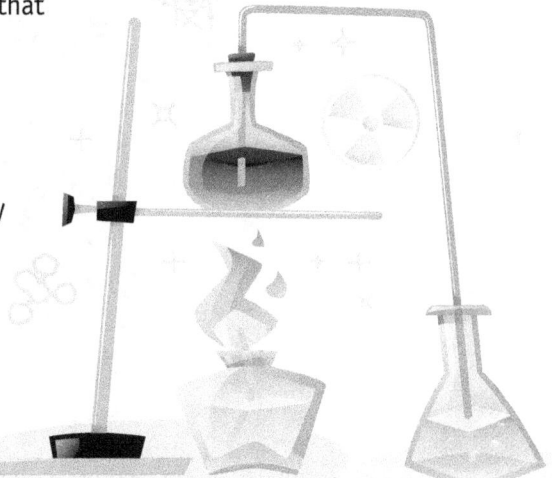

Because of Curie, there is also a new branch of science: the study of radioactivity. Her discovery of radium and its uses changed the way people think about matter and energy. Scientists continue to build on her work.

Curie was afraid her discoveries would be used to make weapons, and her fears were realized when the atomic bomb was made. But her work has also done great good in the world—and that's exactly what she hoped to do.

Name: _____ Date: _____

▢Marie Curie▢ Response

Directions: Reread the text on page 75 to answer each question.

1. Radiation is a form of _____.

   Ⓐ energy

   Ⓑ science

   Ⓒ cancer

   Ⓓ legacy

2. How do people use radiation today?
   _____
   _____

3. How did Marie Curie pay the ultimate price?
   _____
   _____

4. How did Curie leave a remarkable legacy?
   _____
   _____
   _____
   _____

Curie discusses her scientific findings.

Fiction Text Teacher Notes
A Moment of Radiation

	Lesson Steps	Teacher Think Alouds
Ready, Set, Predict!	• Provide students with the poem, and project a larger version for the class to see while you model. • Ask students to work in teams to read the title and predict how the poem might relate to the text about Marie Curie.	
Go!	• Challenge students to read the poem independently, drawing hearts beside each part of the text that shows emotion. • Read the text aloud as students follow along. Demonstrate reading with expression to indicate the author's feelings.	"The author is grateful that Curie's work helps her mom. I can imagine she would feel emotional about this."
Reread to Clarify	• Ask students to circle *–tion* words as they reread the text to clarify. In teams, have students discuss the words' meanings and why the author selected them. How do they contribute to the theme? • Invite students to meet in pairs to discuss the text and its central theme.	"Based on the author's use of the words *castigation* and *detestation*, I wonder if people agreed with Curie."
Reread to Question	• Tell students to reread the text for the purpose of questioning. Ask them to underline at least two sentences and to write questions for the underlined text.	
Reread to Summarize and Respond	• Have partners work together to create four to six sketches that summarize the poem.	

*__Note:__ For more tips, engagement strategies, and fluency options to include in this lesson, see pages 122–128.

A Moment of Radiation

By Andrea Verde

I believe that it is plain to see
Upon this opinion, we can surely agree
Never before was there
      or after will there ever be
A scientist as incredible as Marie Curie
What you did defies explanation
Entire life spent in radiation
At a time when working alone as a scientist
As a woman,
      caused castigation
           detestation
           aggravation
But nevertheless, you showed determination.
I'll stop rhyming for a moment
In this moment
As I sit with my mother
Asleep, free from pain, for the moment
      this moment
I have a moment to get back to my homework
Science
Radiation
You
I've been learning about you
The sacrifices you made
For science, for discovery, for the world
Right now,
      in this moment
           ...for my mom.
The thing that eventually killed you, Marie, has,
      for the moment,
           saved her life.
Radiation could only be understood
      by someone willing to make sacrifices
In your case, the ultimate sacrifice.

Mom gets sick,
Well, more sick
A different sick,
From the treatments.
But she is getting better
      because of radiation
           because of discoveries you made
Your work as a scientist has helped so many people
But right now,
      in this moment,
           I only care about how
what you did
      helped my mom.

Name: _____ Date: _____

"A Moment of Radiation" Response

Directions: Reread the poem on page 78 to answer each question.

1. According to the poet, what kind of sacrifice did Marie Curie make?

   Ⓐ She had to work a lot.
   Ⓑ She spent a lot of time studying.
   Ⓒ Curie's work ended up killing her.
   Ⓓ Curie cured cancer for the poet's mother.

2. Why might it have been a problem for a woman to be a scientist during Curie's lifetime?
   _____
   _____

3. The poet says that Curie's work helped so many people, but what is the poet's main concern?
   _____
   _____
   _____

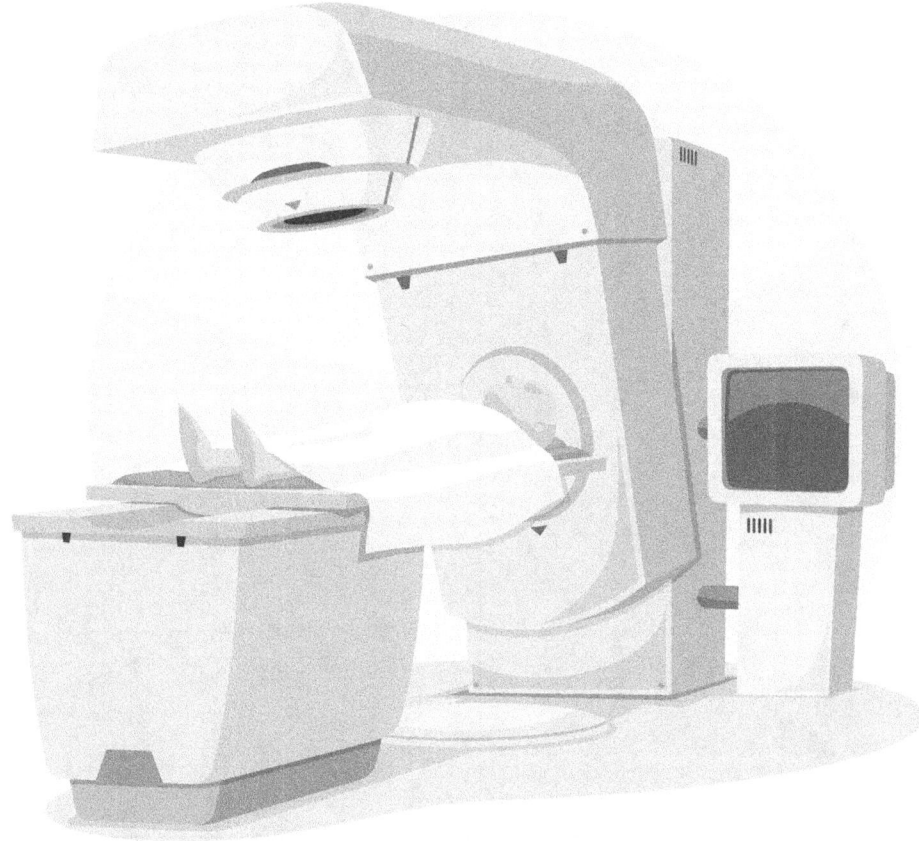

Name: _____ Date: _____

Let's Compare!

Helpful and Harmful

Directions: Complete the chart. Describe how radiation can be helpful and how it can be harmful. Write a paragraph that summarizes how radiation is both helpful and harmful.

Helpful	Harmful

Name:_____ Date:_____

Thinking About Radiation

Directions: Choose at least two of these activities to complete.

Expanding Reading

Reread "A Moment of Radiation." Then research Marie Curie. What was her background? How did she break barriers for women in science? Share your findings with a partner.

Building Fluency

Read "Marie Curie" with a partner. Take turns performing paragraphs. Focus on reading with emotion and expression.

Exploring Words

Reread "A Moment of Radiation," and write phrases that show the poet is grateful to Marie Curie.

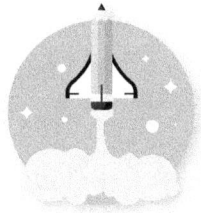

Crafting Writing

Reread "Marie Curie." Write your own poem about Curie and her work with radiation. Use "A Moment of Radiation" as inspiration for your poem.

Unit 9 Overview
Stress

Theme Summary

Stress is a powerful thing. It can bring about positive reactions and it can be harmful. In this lesson, students will read a nonfiction text about the powerful effects of stress. They will also read a poem that illustrates stress and worry.

Answer Key

"The Power of Stress" Response (page 85)

1. C. both beneficial and harmful
2. A. releasing adrenaline and cortisol
3. When there is a major life change, we should take care of ourselves and talk about what we are feeling.
4. A person can deal with stress by eating healthy food, getting plenty of sleep, exercising, and finding ways to relax.

"Good Morning" Response (page 88)

1. D. She overslept.
2. Her mother is concerned because the girl has bruises on her arms and legs.
3. Students may say that her day is going to continue to go poorly. They may say that because she started her day in a frantic way, the rest of her day might go the same.

Let's Compare! Stressed Out! (page 89)

Responses will vary.

We all deal with stress. It can make us feel tired, sluggish, or anxious. Stress can also give us a boost of energy to finish important projects. Some ways to combat stress are getting enough sleep, exercising, and eating healthily. Taking a few minutes to take deep breaths can also help, too. Don't let stress get you down. Take some time to take care of yourself. You'll get through it!

Standards

- Determine a central idea of a text and analyze its development over the course of the text, including how it emerges and is shaped and refined by specific details; provide an objective summary of the text.

- Determine a theme or central idea of a text and how it is conveyed through particular details; provide a summary of the text distinct from personal opinions or judgments.

- Knows the strategies to manage stress and feelings caused by disappointment, separation, or loss (e.g., talking over problems with others, understanding that feelings of isolation and depression will pass, examining the situation leading to the feelings).

Materials

- *The Power of Stress* (page 84)
- *"The Power of Stress" Response* (page 85)
- *"Good Morning"* (page 87)
- *"Good Morning" Response* (page 88)
- *Let's Compare! Stressed Out!* (page 89)
- *Thinking About Stress* (page 90)

Comparing the Texts

After students complete the lessons for each text, have them work in pairs to reread both texts and complete *Let's Compare! Stressed Out!* (page 89). Finally, students can work to complete the *Thinking About Stress* matrix (page 90). The matrix activities allow students to work on important literacy skills of reading, writing, vocabulary, and fluency. For further text analysis, compare these texts to "Fifteen, Maybe Sixteen Things to Worry About" by Judith Viorst.

Nonfiction Text Teacher Notes
The Power of Stress

		Lesson Steps	Teacher Think Alouds
	Ready, Set, Predict!	• Provide the text for students, and display a larger version for the class to see as you model. • Direct students to read the first two sentences of the text. Have them share things that cause them stress in their lives as well as how they manage that stress.	"The first two sentences of the text give me a good idea about its content."
	Go!	• Have students read the text independently, underlining examples of good stress and bad stress. Underline examples of good stress with a green colored pencil and examples of bad stress with a red colored pencil. • Read the text aloud, modeling fluent reading and emphasizing appropriate reading rate.	
	Reread to Clarify	• Have students reread the text to clarify. • Direct students to clarify their understanding of how stress is related to chemical reactions in the body by underlining examples.	"I didn't think about stress being a positive reaction that helps me to be productive and creative."
	Reread to Question	• Have students reread the text in pairs for the purpose of questioning. Direct each student to write two questions that can be answered from the text. Have students discuss answers. • Have students respond to the questions and prompts on page 85.	
	Reread to Summarize and Respond	• Instruct students to reread the text to summarize. Have them create T-charts with positive aspects of stress on one side and negative aspects on the other. Students should share their summaries with partners.	

*Note: For more tips, engagement strategies, and fluency options to include in this lesson, see pages 122–128.

The Power of Stress

By Wendy Conklin

You might hear your friends describe themselves as "stressed out," and you may sometimes feel that way, too. Stress is an unavoidable part of life, and it can come in many different forms. But have you ever thought of stress as a good thing? Think about it—everyone lives with low-level stress. You might have responsibilities such as mowing the lawn, finishing homework, or walking the dog. These small stressors of everyday life help you develop a sense of responsibility.

Stress can also set in because of deadlines—the nagging things that we have to complete by certain times. Deadlines help people get things done while also forcing people to solve problems and think creatively in a given amount of time. If we had all the time in the world, we might not get anything done, so sometimes stress is a good motivator. Remember that while some stress is normal, even helpful, it's important to ask for support if you are feeling overwhelmed.

Then, there's the stress that arises from a major life change. During these big life changes, such as changing schools or recovering from a serious illness, it's especially important to take care of yourself. You might also talk through your feelings with a trustworthy friend or adult.

Have you ever experienced an emergency that caused your heart to race and made you feel like you had superhuman strength? That was your adrenal gland producing a hormone called *adrenaline*. When you are under stress, your brain produces a variety of chemicals, including adrenaline, that go through the bloodstream to other parts of your body. Simultaneously, the adrenal glands also produce a hormone called *cortisol*. This gives your muscles and brain the energy to react as needed to the situation. When the stress ends, the cortisol travels back to the brain and tells it to stop producing the stress hormones. Then, your body is supposed to go back to normal.

For some people, however, this stress does not end. As a result, they experience health problems, such as panic attacks or trouble sleeping. It's important to learn to manage stress so that you don't experience the negative effects of it. Be sure to eat healthy foods, get enough sleep, exercise, and find healthy ways to relax, such as breathing techniques or meditation. If you still have trouble, be sure to talk to your doctor about your stress levels.

Name:_____ Date:_____

"The Power of Stress" Response

Directions: Reread the text on page 84 to answer each question.

1. Stress can be _____.

   Ⓐ beneficial

   Ⓑ harmful

   Ⓒ both beneficial and harmful

   Ⓓ relaxing

2. How does the human body react to stress?

   Ⓐ releasing adrenaline and cortisol

   Ⓑ releasing endorphins

   Ⓒ having a panic attack

   Ⓓ craving healthy foods

3. What are ways to deal with the stress of a major life change?
   _____
   _____

4. What can a person do to deal with ongoing stress?
   _____
   _____
   _____

© Shell Education

51735—Close Reading with Paired Texts

85

Fiction Text Teacher Notes
Good Morning

	Lesson Steps	Teacher Think Alouds
Ready, Set, Predict!	• Provide students with the text and project a larger version for the class to see. • Have students read the title and predict how the poem might relate to stress. Students should share their predictions about the poem with partners or in teams.	"I see that the title is 'Good Morning' and I see an alarm clock. I know that the other text was about stress so this makes me think that 'Good Morning' isn't really going to be about a good morning."
Go!	• Have students read the text independently. Direct them to draw stars next to any parts of the text that remind them of their own lives. • Read the text aloud as students follow along. Model the use of appropriate expression to express the narrator's worry.	"Think about how the narrator's voice might sound if she feels stressed out."
Reread to Clarify	• Have students reread the poem, underlining the places where the mother is "speaking." • Instruct them to meet with partners to discuss how they know who is "speaking" in each part of the poem.	
Reread to Question	• Tell students to reread the text for the purpose of questioning. Have them ask, "Could this happen? If so, how could it be handled?" • Have students meet in pairs to share their answers to the questions.	
Reread to Summarize and Respond	• Ask partners to work together to summarize the poem in one paragraph. Direct them to include the real reason the girl is so stressed out. • Students should then share their summaries with other pairs of students.	

*Note: For more tips, engagement strategies, and fluency options to include in this lesson, see pages 122–128.

Good Morning

By Voiza Maxwell

Oh my gosh, what is that sound?
    "Hey! Wake up! Come on down!"
Oh no! What time? What about my alarm!
    "Power went out last night. What's that on your arm?"
Mom! Stop! I'm going to be late!
    "Seriously, honey? It's not even eight."
But I have swim practice! This isn't right!
    "Maybe you shouldn't have stayed up last night."
Ugh, Mom, leave me alone
    "It's just that…"
Ack! Where is my phone?
    "Sweetie, please, come have some eggs."
I'm not hungry
    "What's that on your leg?"
It's nothing, Mom. I'm sorry, okay?
    "They look like bruises…"
Mom, hey!
I don't feel great,
I can't find my phone,
I'm totally late,
The power went out,
No alarm went off,
I don't mean to shout!
Just please don't scoff,
I didn't get enough sleep,
My homework's not done,
My boyfriend's a creep,
I know I'm not the only one,
Who's ever overslept,
    "But…"
Please, I'm not done,
I feel overwhelmed,
I might have to quit,
    "You're not being yourself."
Now I have a new zit!
The bruises are from basketball,
With swimming and dancing, and one or two falls,
I'm doing a lot, and I know you're proud,
But most of the time,
I just feel stressed out.
    "So…no eggs?"

Name: _____   Date: _____

"Good Morning" Response

Directions: Reread the text on page 87 to answer each question.

1. What was the primary reason that this girl is stressed out in this poem?

   Ⓐ She has a zit on her face. Ⓒ She's not feeling well.

   Ⓑ She can't find her phone. Ⓓ She overslept.

2. What is the girl's mother concerned about in the poem?
   _____
   _____

3. How might the rest of this person's day go? Why do you think that?
   _____
   _____
   _____

Name: _____ Date: _____

Let's Compare!
Stressed Out!

Directions: Reread both texts. Write a blog post about the negative effects of stress and worry. Give some ideas for managing stress and worry.

Name: _____   Date: _____

Thinking About Stress

Directions: Choose at least two of these activities to complete.

 ## Expanding Reading

Reread "The Power of Stress." Write a note in the margin about a fact that surprised you. Then find another article online about how stress affects the body. With a partner, create a poster about how to combat stress in your lives.

 ## Building Fluency

Read "Good Morning" with a partner. Take turns reading stanzas. Think about how a person speaks rapidly when he or she is nervous or worried. Focus on reading in a manner that reflects the girl's feelings.

 ## Exploring Words

Review "The Power of Stress." Create a list of words that you do not usually use in day-to-day conversation. Pair up with a partner to discuss the text. Use five of the words on your list in the conversation.

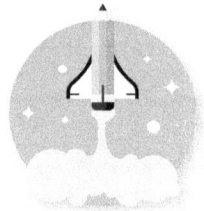 ## Crafting Writing

Positive self-talk is a great way to deal with worry and stress. Review "Good Morning," and respond to the girl with the positive statements. Examples: *Take a deep breath. You'll feel better if you eat something. Don't get upset with your mom, she is just worried about you.*

Unit 10 Overview
Equal Rights

Theme Summary

Equal rights has been a critical issue throughout history and students will learn the importance of embracing the rights of all people. In this pair of texts, students will read about the 1963 March on Washington and a poem about a slave's cry for freedom. This text pair is sure to inspire strong feelings about human rights.

Standards

- Compare and contrast texts in different forms or genres (e.g., stories and poems; historical novels and fantasy stories) in terms of their approaches to similar themes and topics.
- Cite textual evidence to support analysis of what the text says explicitly as well as inferences drawn from the text.
- Understands the struggle for racial and gender equality and for the extension of civil liberties.

Materials

- *March on Washington* (pages 93–94)
- "March on Washington" Response (page 94)
- *On Liberty and Slavery* (page 96)
- "On Liberty and Slavery" Response (page 97)
- *Let's Compare! Human Rights* (page 98)
- *Thinking About Equal Rights* (page 99)

Comparing the Texts

After students complete the lessons for each text, have them work in pairs to reread both texts and complete *Let's Compare! Human Rights* (page 98). Finally, students can work to complete the *Thinking About Equal Rights* matrix (page 99). The matrix activities allow students to work on important literacy skills of reading, writing, vocabulary, and fluency. For further text analysis, compare these texts to "I, Too" by Langston Hughes.

Answer Key

"March on Washington" Response (page 94)

1. D. to show that the treatment of African Americans was still unfair
2. It means that he spoke what he was feeling and he spoke about things that were important to him.
3. In his speech, he mentioned white men, Jewish people, Gentiles, Protestants, and Catholics. He didn't just speak about African Americans.

"On Liberty and Slavery" Response (page 97)

1. B. deprived of liberty
2. Responses may include: Will I ever be without pain and sadness before I die?
3. Responses may include: *cheerful sound, joyful trump of peace*

Let's Compare! Human Rights (page 98)

Responses may vary.

	March on Washington	On Liberty and Slavery
What did the people want? / What did the person want?	equal rights, decent housing, more jobs, freedom	liberty, freedom from pain, freedom from sadness, freedom from slavery
What was the mood of the March? / What was the mood of the poem?	excitement	sadness
What is the hope of the people? / What is the hope of the narrator?	that all people will be united and free at last	to be free from slavery

Nonfiction Text Teacher Notes
March on Washington

Social Studies Texts

	Lesson Steps	**Teacher Think Alouds**
Ready, Set, Predict!	• Begin by having students share what they know about the civil rights movement. Tell students they will read a nonfiction text about an important event in history. • Ask students to share what they know about Martin Luther King Jr. and his quest for equal rights with partners. • Have students make predictions about the content of the "March on Washington" text based on the title and headings and share their predictions in groups of three.	
Go!	• Provide the text for students, and display a larger version for the class to see while you model. • Have students read the text independently, underlining the main idea of each paragraph. • Read the text aloud, modeling fluent reading. As you read, increase the loudness of your voice to emphasize the building excitement of the event.	
Reread to Clarify	• Have students reread the text to clarify anything confusing. • Ask students to circle any words that need to be clarified. Have them share in groups of three to discuss the words' meanings.	"If I need to clarify the meaning of the word *orate*, I can think of how it is used in the sentence. It says the leaders took the stage to *orate* about civil rights, so I think it means *speak* or *give a speech*."
Reread to Question	• Have students reread the text in pairs for the purpose of asking questions. Direct each student to write a question about the event. Have pairs discuss the questions and determine the answers, using evidence from the text. • Have students respond to the questions and prompts on page 94.	"This event happened in August and the people were in a huge crowd. My question about the setting is, 'Was it really hot that day?' How might the weather have affected the mood of the marchers?"
Reread to Summarize and Respond	• Share a video of Martin Luther King Jr.'s "I Have a Dream" speech. Instruct students to reread the text to summarize, underlining important points. Have students use their underlined sentences, the headings, and what they saw in the "I Have a Dream" speech to write their summaries. Share in groups.	

*Note: For more tips, engagement strategies, and fluency options to include in this lesson, see pages 122–128.

March on Washington

By Torrey Maloof

Typically, the city streets are quiet in the early morning hours in Washington, DC, but that is not the case today, August 28, 1963. Buses are inundating the city at a feverish pace, and the smell of diesel exhaust is thick in the air as bus after bus heads to the heart of the nation's capital. These buses are carrying eager and committed citizens who want to do their part to make a difference. They don't want to witness history. They want to change history, and today they will.

African Americans aren't the only ones walking; there are white people, too. There are elderly people in wheelchairs and young children being pushed in strollers. People of all ages, ethnicities, and creeds have come together for this one extraordinary event. A sense of unity and excitement fills the air with each passing step.

Meeting at the Monument

Nearing the Washington Monument, it becomes virtually impossible to maneuver through the throng of people. Premade picket signs with writing demanding equal rights, decent housing, and more jobs are handed out among the crowd. An announcement is made stating that 90,000 people have arrived, and there are still more coming. Demonstrators roar with excitement, and the atmosphere becomes electric.

Time to March

The trek to the Lincoln Memorial is scheduled to begin at 11:30 a.m. and covers almost two miles. As they march, some groups sing hymns while others chant, "Freedom! Freedom!" Numerous civil rights leaders and activists take to the stage and orate on the importance of the fight for civil rights and equality.

Speaking for Change

To the side of the stage stands Dr. Martin Luther King Jr. Before he takes the podium, African American vocalist Mahalia Jackson sings. Her commanding voice carries an old slave spiritual to the masses. "I been 'buked and I been scorned / I'm gonna tell my Lord / When I get home / Just how long you've been treating me wrong." The wild cheering and chanting slowly die down as King begins to speak into the microphone.

At first when King speaks, he reads his words from a paper, but before long he discards his prepared words and speaks from his heart. His cadence grabs the crowd's full attention. He speaks for 17 minutes as he delivers his "I Have a Dream" speech.

The Washington Monument was completed in 1884.

Name:_____ Date: _____

March on Washington (cont)

When we allow freedom to ring— when we let it ring from every city and every hamlet, from every state and every city, we will be able to speed up that day when all of God's children, black men and white men, Jews and Gentiles, Protestants and Catholics, will be able to join hands and sing in the words of the old Negro spiritual, "Free at last, Free at last, Great God a-mighty, We are free at last."

Reflection

The persuasive and powerful speeches given by the movement's greatest civil rights leaders have inspired and energized a nation to take action. Washington and the world at large will never be the same. The air is thick with hopes and dreams, and change is firmly planted on the horizon. The March on Washington for Jobs and Freedom has come to a triumphant culmination.

□March on Washington□ Response

Directions: Reread the text on pages 93–94 to answer each question.

1. Why did the vocalist sing an old slave spiritual?

   Ⓐ It was a pretty song.

   Ⓑ It was a song she had written.

   Ⓒ The people at the march asked her to sing the song.

   Ⓓ To show that the treatment of African Americans was still unfair.

2. What does it mean that Martin Luther King Jr. *speaks from his heart*?
   _____
   _____

3. What clues in the text indicate that Dr. King wanted equal rights for everyone and not just for African Americans?
   _____
   _____
   _____

Fiction Text Teacher Notes
On Liberty and Slavery

	Lesson Steps	Teacher Think Alouds
Ready, Set, Predict!	• Provide students with the poem "On Liberty and Slavery," and display a larger version for the class to see. • Have students read the title and predict how the poem might relate to the text about the March on Washington. Then ask them to think about what they know about slavery. • Have students do quick writes of their predictions. Then they can switch papers with a partner to share their thoughts.	
Go!	• Have students read the poem independently, underlining phrases that show the author is miserable. • Read the text aloud as students follow along. Read slowly with clear pauses at the ends of lines to emphasize the author's anguish.	"The narrator is an enslaved person who wants freedom. I need to read the poem slowly and sadly to communicate how he feels."
Reread to Clarify	• Ask students to reread the poem to clarify. Instruct them to circle words and phrases that need to be clarified. • Have students meet in pairs to discuss the words they circled and ways to determine their meanings by reading and using context.	"The word *quell* is new to me, so I need to clarify. He says he needs to soothe the pain, which means stop the pain. So *quell the grief* probably means *stop the grief*."
Reread to Question	• Tell students to reread the text for the purpose of questioning. Direct them to ask questions they might ask the author. • Have students meet in pairs to share their questions and discuss answers.	"What does it mean when you (the author) say *Slavery hide her haggard face?*"
Reread to Summarize and Respond	• Have partners work together to summarize the poem in one sentence.	"The writer of the poem says a lot about slavery and freedom, but how can we summarize this in just one sentence?"

*Note: For more tips, engagement strategies, and fluency options to include in this lesson, see pages 122–128.

On Liberty and Slavery

by George Moses Horton

Alas! and am I born for this,
    To wear this slavish chain?
Deprived of all created bliss,
    Through hardship, toil, and pain!

How long have I in bondage lain,
    And languished to be free!
Alas! and must I still complain—
    Deprived of liberty.

Oh, Heaven! and is there no relief
    This side the silent grave—
To soothe the pain--to quell the grief
    And anguish of a slave?

Come, Liberty, thou cheerful sound,
    Roll through my ravished ears!
Come, let my grief in joys be drowned,
    And drive away my fears.

Say unto foul oppression, Cease:
    Ye tyrants rage no more,
And let the joyful trump of peace,
    Now bid the vassal soar.

Soar on the pinions of that dove
    Which long has cooed for thee,
And breathed her notes from Afric's grove,
    The sound of Liberty.

Oh, Liberty! thou golden prize,
    So often sought by blood—
We crave thy sacred sun to rise,
    The gift of nature's God!

Bid Slavery hide her haggard face,
    And barbarism fly:
I scorn to see the sad disgrace
    In which enslaved I lie.

Dear Liberty! upon thy breast,
    I languish to respire;
And like the Swan upon her nest,
    I'd to thy smiles retire.

Oh, blest asylum--heavenly balm!
    Unto thy boughs I flee—
And in thy shades the storm shall calm,
    With songs of Liberty!

Name:_____ Date:_____

"On Liberty and Slavery" Response

Directions: Reread the text on page 96 to answer each question.

1. Which of the following phrases from the text means *prevented from having freedom?*

    Ⓐ breathed her notes

    Ⓑ deprived of liberty

    Ⓒ sought by blood

    Ⓓ crave thy sacrifice

2. Write one sentence that summarizes the third stanza of the poem.
   _____
   _____

3. How does the poet describe liberty?
   _____
   _____
   _____

© Shell Education   51735—Close Reading with Paired Texts   97

Name:_____ Date:_____

Let's Compare!

Human Rights

Directions: Reread both texts. Use information from both texts to complete the chart.

March on Washington	On Liberty and Slavery
What did the people want?	**What did the person want?**
What was the mood of the March?	**What was the mood of the poem?**
What is the hope of the people?	**What is the hope of the narrator?**

Name: _____ Date: _____

Thinking About Equal Rights

Directions: Choose at least two of these activities to complete.

Expanding Reading

Reread "March on Washington." Write a note in the margin that explains the difference between the message of Mahalia Jackson's song and the message of Dr. King's speech.

Building Fluency

In a group of three, practice reading "On Liberty and Slavery." Take turns reading stanzas, and read the last one together. Increase voice loudness on stanzas with exclamation marks. Decrease loudness on other stanzas. In groups of three, find the words to Martin Luther King Jr.'s "I Have a Dream" speech. Then practice performing excerpts of the speech. Change your tone, expression, and volume to convey meaning.

Exploring Words

Review "On Liberty and Slavery." Create a list of words that communicate sadness. Then, make a list of words that communicate happiness. Put the words in order from sad to happy.

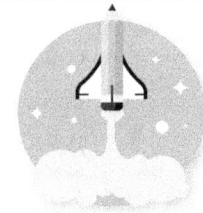

Crafting Writing

A letter to the editor expresses an opinion about an issue. It is addressed to the editor (Dear Editor), but is meant for the public to read in a newspaper or magazine. Using the nonfiction and fiction texts as inspiration, write a letter to the editor, expressing your opinions about equal rights for all people. For inspiration, use the Internet to search for editorials about freedom and equal rights.

Unit 11 Overview
Women's Suffrage

Theme Summary

The word *suffrage* means *the right to vote in political elections*. Before 1920, women did not have the right to vote in the United States. In the early 1900s, women across the nation stood up against these beliefs and fought, successfully, for the right to vote. With this text pair, students will read an excerpt of a speech to Congress about women's suffrage. They will also read a passage that displays the view of women at that time in history.

Answer Key

Excerpt from *Address to Congress on Women's Suffrage* Response (page 103)

1. D. You claim to want women to have the right to vote.

2. She says that women will eventually be able to vote. If a party tries to fight them now, women will vote against them later. She wants to know if that risk is worth it to them.

3. Responses may include: *The woman's hour has struck*, *The idea will not perish, ... and when the party or parties which have so delayed woman's suffrage finally let it come*, or *woman's suffrage is coming—you know it*.

Introduction to *Are Women People?* Response (page 106)

1. B. legislator

2. He doesn't think a woman should have the right to vote.

3. The poet is showing us how hypocritical men were during the early 1900s.

Let's Compare! A Woman's Right to Vote (page 107)

Tweets will vary.

Women are citizens, too. They deserve the right to vote just as much as any man. Women should be treated fairly. Women are equal to men! For years, men ruled the government. That stops now. Let women have a voice! #womensrights #womenshouldvotetoo #womenareequal

Standards

→ Determine a central idea of a text and analyze its development over the course of the text, including how it emerges and is shaped and refined by specific details; provide an objective summary of the text.

→ Write informative/explanatory texts to examine a topic and convey ideas, concepts, and information through the selection, organization, and analysis of relevant content.

→ Understands the struggle for racial and gender equality and for the extension of civil liberties.

Materials

→ *Excerpt from* Address to Congress on Women's Suffrage (page 102)

→ *Excerpt from* Address to Congress on Women's Suffrage *Response* (page 103)

→ *Introduction to* Are Women People? (page 105)

→ *Introduction to* Are Women People? *Response* (page 106)

→ *Let's Compare! A Woman's Right to Vote* (page 107)

→ *Thinking About Women's Suffrage* (page 108)

Comparing the Texts

After students complete the lessons for each text, have them work in pairs to reread both texts and complete *Let's Compare! A Woman's Right to Vote* (page 107). Finally, students can work to complete the *Thinking About Women's Suffrage* matrix (page 108). The matrix activities allow students to work on important literacy skills of reading, writing, vocabulary, and fluency.

Nonfiction Text Teacher Notes
Excerpt from *Address to Congress on Women's Suffrage*

	Lesson Steps	Teacher Think Alouds
Ready, Set, Predict!	• Tell students they will read a speech to Congress in 1916 making a case for women's suffrage (the right to vote). Share some basic background information about Carrie Chapman Catt. • Have students make predictions about why the speech was given and share their predictions in pairs.	
Go!	• Provide the text for students, and display a larger version for the class to see while you model. • Have students read the text independently, putting stars beside key details in the speech. • Read the text aloud, modeling fluent reading. As you read, demonstrate the use of word or phrase repetition to emphasize points.	"In the second paragraph, I am going to repeat the phrase, *to beg men who cannot read*. By repeating this phrase, I emphasize the absurdity of an educated woman asking an uneducated man if she can vote."
Reread to Clarify	• Have students reread the text, underlining words or phrases that might be confusing. • Direct students to circle any words that need to be clarified. Have them share in groups of three to discuss the words' meanings and strategies for figuring out the definition. Did they use context clues? Did they analyze parts of the word?	"If I need to clarify the meaning of the word *enfranchisement*, I can think of how it is used in the sentence. It says women resent the delay of *enfranchisement*, so it probably refers to the right to vote."
Reread to Question	• Have students reread the text in pairs for the purpose of asking questions. Direct each student to write a question about women's suffrage that begins with "Why do you think..." Pairs then discuss the questions and determine the answers. • Have students respond to the questions and prompts on page 103.	
Reread to Summarize and Respond	• Instruct students to reread the text to summarize. Have them use their underlined details to write summaries and share in groups. Invite students to share their favorite facts and why they choose those facts.	

*Note: For more tips, engagement strategies, and fluency options to include in this lesson, see pages 122–128.

Excerpt from *Address to Congress on Women's Suffrage*

By Carrie Chapman Catt

Do you realize that in no other country in the world with democratic tendencies is suffrage so completely denied as in a considerable number of our own states? There are thirteen black states where no suffrage for women exists, and fourteen others where suffrage for women is more limited than in many foreign countries.

Do you realize that… you drive women of education, refinement, achievement, to beg men who cannot read for their political freedom? Do you realize that such anomalies as a college president asking her janitor to give her a vote are overstraining the patience and driving women to desperation? Do you realize that women in increasing numbers indignantly resent the long delay in their enfranchisement?

Your party platforms have pledged women suffrage. Then why not be honest, frank friends of our cause, adopt it in reality as your own, make it a party program, and "fight with us"? As a party measure, a measure of all parties, why not put the amendment through Congress and the legislatures? We shall all be better friends, we shall have a happier nation, we women will be free to support loyally the party of our choice, and we shall be far prouder of our history.

"There is one thing mightier than kings and armies"—aye, than Congresses and political parties—"the power of an idea when its time has come to move." The time for woman suffrage has come. The woman's hour has struck. If parties prefer to postpone action longer and thus do battle with this idea, they challenge the inevitable. The idea will not perish; the party which opposes it may. Every delay, every trick, every political dishonesty from now on will antagonize the women of the land more and more, and when the party or parties which have so delayed woman suffrage finally let it come, their sincerity will be doubted and their appeal to the new voters will be met with suspicion. This is the psychology of the situation. Can you afford the risk? Think it over.

Gentlemen, we hereby petition you, our only designated representatives, to redress our grievances by the immediate passage of the Federal Suffrage Amendment and to use your influence to secure its ratification in your own state, in order that the women of our nation may be endowed with political freedom before the next presidential election, and that our nation may resume its world leadership in democracy.

Woman suffrage is coming—you know it. Will you, Honorable Senators and Members of the House of Representatives, help or hinder it?

Name: _____ Date: _____

Excerpt from *Address to Congress on Women's Suffrage* Response

Directions: Reread the text on page 102 to answer each question.

1. What does Carrie Chapman Catt mean when she says, *Your party platforms have pledged women suffrage*?

   Ⓐ You made a promise to women, and you broke it.

   Ⓑ Women stand on platforms to say they want to vote.

   Ⓒ Other people in your party want women to vote.

   Ⓓ You claim to want women to have the right to vote.

2. Explain *the risk* Catt speaks of in the fourth paragraph.
   _____
   _____
   _____

3. Which statements does Catt make to show she is confident that women will have the right to vote eventually?
   _____
   _____
   _____

Women fight for their right to vote.

Fiction Text Teacher Notes
Introduction to *Are Women People?*

	Lesson Steps	Teacher Think Alouds
Ready, Set, Predict!	• Provide students with the introduction to *Are Women People?* and display a larger version for the class to see. • Have students read the title and predict how the poem might relate to women's suffrage. Have students meet in small groups to talk briefly about their predictions.	
Go!	• Have students read the text independently, underlining the two different answers to the question, *Are women people?* • Read the text aloud as students follow along. Read with expression to indicate lines spoken by the boy and those spoken by the father.	"The father has two different answers to the question. At first, he says women are not people and then he says they are, so now I need to reread to figure out what he means."
Reread to Clarify	• Direct students to reread the excerpt to clarify. Instruct them to circle words or phrases that need clarification. • Ask students to meet in pairs to discuss the words they circled and ways to clarify them.	
Reread to Question	• Tell students to reread the text for the purpose of questioning. Direct them to ask questions about the message of the text. They may use the prompts I wonder why... or I wonder how... • Have students meet in pairs to share their questions and discuss answers.	"I wonder why the issue of money changed the father's answer about women being people?"
Reread to Summarize and Respond	• Have partners work together to summarize the excerpt in two sentences.	"The father communicates two different messages about women. I will summarize the two messages in two different sentences."

*****Note:** For more tips, engagement strategies, and fluency options to include in this lesson, see pages 122–128.

51735—*Close Reading with Paired Texts*   © Shell Education

Introduction to *Are Women People?*

Are Women People? A Book of Rhymes for Suffrage Times
by Alice Duer Miller

Father, what is a Legislature?
A representative body elected by the people of the state.
Are women people?
No, my son, criminals, lunatics and women are not people.
Do legislators legislate for nothing?
Oh, no; they are paid a salary.
By whom?
By the people.
Are women people?
Of course, my son, just as much as men are.

Name:_____ Date:_____

Introduction to *Are Women People?* Response

Directions: Reread the text on page 105 to answer each question.

1. Which of the following is an elected person who represents people?

   Ⓐ a criminal   Ⓒ a woman

   Ⓑ a legislator   Ⓓ a man

2. What would be a reason the father does not consider a woman a person?
   _____
   _____

3. What is the lesson the poet is trying to teach us?
   _____
   _____
   _____

Name:_____ Date:_____

Let's Compare!
A Woman's Right to Vote

Directions: Reread both texts. Use the information from the texts to write a tweet defending or rebutting women's suffrage. You must summarize your thoughts in 50 words or less. You may use no more than three hashtags.

Name:_____ Date:_____

Thinking About Women's Suffrage

Directions: Choose at least two of these activities to complete.

Expanding Reading

Reread the excerpt from the *Address to Congress on Women's Suffrage*. Then do some research on a famous American woman from the suffrage movement. Give a brief oral presentation on information from your research.

Building Fluency

In pairs, practice reading the Introduction to *Are Women People? A Book of Rhymes for Suffrage Times*. Designate one person to read the father's lines and one to read the son's lines. Focus on the use of expression. Then, record and share your reading.

Exploring Words

Review the excerpt from the *Address to Congress on Women's Suffrage*. Create a list of words or phrases the authors uses as an imperative. An imperative is a command.

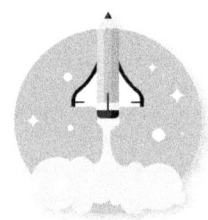

Crafting Writing

Imagine you are fighting for something in which you believe strongly. Create a poster with a catchy headline. Briefly state your argument and how you want others to participate in the cause. Include illustrations that represent particular points.

Unit 12 Overview
The Devastation of War

Theme Summary

There have been many historic events in the world involving war. In this lesson, students will get a glimpse of World War II and the Civil War. They will read a nonfiction text about the bombing of Pearl Harbor, which marked when the United States entered World War II. They will also read a fiction text that captures a snapshot of a battle during the Civil War.

Standards

- Determine a central idea of a text and analyze its development over the course of the text, including how it emerges and is shaped and refined by specific details; provide an objective summary of the text.
- Determine a theme or central idea of a text and how it is conveyed through particular details; provide a summary of the text distinct from personal opinions or judgments.
- Understands that war has an impact on shaping the United States.

Materials

- *Pearl Harbor* (pages 111–112)
- "Pearl Harbor" *Response* (page 112)
- Excerpt from *The Guns of Bull Run* (page 114)
- Excerpt from *The Guns of Bull Run Response* (page 115)
- *Let's Compare! Pearl Harbor vs. Bull Run* (page 116)
- *Thinking About the Devastation of War* (page 117)

Comparing the Texts

After students complete the lessons for each text, have them work in pairs to reread both texts and complete *Let's Compare! Pearl Harbor vs. Bull Run* (page 116). Finally, students can work to complete the *Thinking About the Devastation of War* matrix (page 117). The matrix activities allow students to work on important literacy skills of reading, writing, vocabulary, and fluency. For further text analysis, compare these texts to "The Waste Land" by T.S. Eliot.

Answer Key

"Pearl Harbor" Response (page 112)

1. B. swarm
2. The devastation was severe because the U.S. military was caught off guard. Ships sunk, thousands of people died and were injured.
3. They don't want anything like that to happen again.

Excerpt from *The Guns of Bull Run* Response (page 115)

1. D. The sun is as red as fire!
2. He starts to breathe hard because he feels nervous with anticipation.
3. He doesn't want to see all of the soldiers being shot.

Let's Compare! Pearl Harbor vs. Bull Run (page 116)

Pearl Harbor	Bull Run
Describe the setting before the attack. a harbor in Hawai'i; ships in the water; soldiers doing daily routines; cloudy sky	**Describe the setting before the attack.** a field in Virginia; early morning; bright sun; soldiers cooking; breakfast over fires
How prepared were they? They were not prepared. They had no idea the Japanese were going to attack them.	**How prepared were they?** The soldiers knew the Northerners were coming. They saw the dust in the air and hid in the grass.
What do we learn about the military men and women? We know that they were doing their daily routines. We also learn that thousands of them were killed or injured.	**What do we learn about the military men?** We learn that the soldiers were young and probably nervous. They were prepared to fight and confident they would win.

© Shell Education   51735—Close Reading with Paired Texts   109

Nonfiction Text Teacher Notes
Pearl Harbor

	Lesson Steps	Teacher Think Alouds
Ready, Set, Predict!	• Tell students they will read a nonfiction text about the bombing of Pearl Harbor. Ask students to share what they already know about the attack on Pearl Harbor. • Have students make predictions about what they might learn about this historic event and share their predictions in pairs.	"At this time, the United States was not fighting in World War II. The attack at Pearl Harbor was what caused the United States to enter the war."
Go!	• Provide the text for students, and display a larger version to use for modeling what to write. • Have students read the text independently, underlining the main idea of each paragraph. • Read the text aloud, modeling fluent reading. As you read, demonstrate the use of voice intensity to emphasize dramatic elements of the story.	"When I get to the fourth paragraph, I will speak with more intensity and then even more in the fifth paragraph where it says *The sky explodes!*"
Reread to Clarify	• Have students reread the text to clarify words and ideas that they might need to explain if discussing the text with a younger student. • Ask students to circle any words that need to be clarified. Have them share in groups of three to discuss the words' meanings and strategies for figuring out the words.	
Reread to Question	• Have students reread the text in pairs for the purpose of asking questions. Direct each student to write a question about the Pearl Harbor attack. Pairs then discuss the questions and determine the answers. • Direct students to respond to the questions and prompts on page 112.	"When I read the second paragraph, I wonder why the military is prepared for war, even though they didn't plan to fight. As I read, I realize that the United States did not have a choice after the attack, so being prepared to fight back was important."
Reread to Summarize and Respond	• Instruct students to reread the text to summarize. Have them use the underlined sentence in each paragraph to write the summary. Ask students to take turns pausing after each paragraph and paraphrasing what it was about. Partners must also work together to underline important facts in each paragraph.	

*Note: For more tips, engagement strategies, and fluency options to include in this lesson, see pages 122–128.

Name: _____   Date: _____

Pearl Harbor

By Dona Herweck Rice

The sun rises over the calm and quiet United States Naval Base at Pearl Harbor on the island of O'ahu, Hawai'i. It is Sunday, and many of the military men and women are on leave for the weekend. Most offices and shops are closed. Still, the base hums as the military personnel stationed there go about their daily routines, whether servicing the vessels and planes that are critical to U.S. military strength or simply enjoying some much-deserved leisure.

The U.S. military is growing in strength, developing the means and training to protect and defend the nation it serves. Knowing that wars are being waged brutally in Europe and the Pacific, U.S. armed forces are prepared, despite the nation's desire to stay isolated from the wars that seemingly have little to do with its concerns. The military is ready to deploy if it needs to. But government leaders are clear: this is not America's war.

On this day, the necessary staff of sailors, soldiers, mechanics, nurses, and service people is at work bright and early, doing their duty for the country they serve. In the military, you can rely on people and systems operating as expected. It's fundamental and essential. The men and women at Pearl Harbor certainly know this to be true.

Except on this day—December 7, 1941—it isn't. An unexpected sound breaks through the familiar clangs and hums of the station. At 7:40 a.m., the swarm of bombers, torpedo planes, and fighter planes approach the island in the Pacific. The 183 aircrafts hide above a layer of clouds to approach O'ahu unseen. The massive, unexpected, and harrowing air strike begins.

The sky explodes! Bombs fall in a devastating firestorm. Just minutes later, the worst devastation comes not only in the destruction of aircraft and ships, but also in loss of life—loss in staggering numbers. A bomb designed to pierce armor is dropped from above and easily rips through the battleship *Arizona*. A massive amount of gunpowder ignites, shooting an explosive fireball through the ship and into the air. The United States ship (USS) *Arizona* is sunk within minutes, killing 1,177 sailors and marines. Many were trapped by both fire and sea. The devastation to the men and women of Pearl Harbor is severe. In all, more than 2,403 people die and more than 1,178 are wounded.

U.S.S. *Neosho* escapes Japanese attackers on December 7, 1941

In addition to the USS *Arizona*, the USS *Utah* and the USS *Oklahoma* were also destroyed. But every other struck vessel—even those that sunk—will eventually be lifted out of the water and repaired to sail again. In fact, many are instrumental in the eventual American defeat of the Japanese after many years of devastating war.

Name: _____ Date: _____

Pearl Harbor (cont.)

The United States was involved in the war until the very end. After atom bombs create unmatched devastation and loss of life in the Japanese cities of Hiroshima and Nagasaki in August 1945, the war comes to an end. The Japanese signed the surrender papers. The streets of the United States—and the base at Pearl Harbor—erupt in celebration.

It has been many years since the attack on Pearl Harbor. Millions of visitors pay tribute at the memorial each year, including countless Japanese tourists. In the end, the attack on Pearl Harbor proved devastating for all, Americans and Japanese alike. Peace between the nations has reigned since the last shots of the war were fired. Today, the nations are allies. But it is important that the lessons of Pearl Harbor and the war are never forgotten.

▫Pearl Harbor▫ Response

Directions: Reread the text on pages 111–112 to answer each question.

1. What word does the author use to help the reader visualize how the bombers and planes looked as they filled the skies over Pearl Harbor?

   Ⓐ clangs   Ⓒ military

   Ⓑ swarm   Ⓓ explosive

2. How severe was the devastation at Pearl Harbor?

   _____
   _____
   _____
   _____

3. Why do Japanese tourists come to pay tribute at the Pearl Harbor memorial?

   _____
   _____
   _____
   _____
   _____

Fiction Text Teacher Notes
Excerpt from *The Guns of Bull Run*

		Lesson Steps	Teacher Think Alouds
	Ready, Set, Predict!	• Have students read the title, quickly skim the text, and predict what the excerpt is about. Also, have them predict why the author wrote the text in this format. Direct students to meet in small groups to talk about their predictions. • Provide students with the text, and display a larger version to use for modeling. Explain that the text is a fictional story about a real event in history—one of two battles at Bull Run.	
	Go!	• Have students read the text independently, underlining parts of the text that help them visualize the setting. • Read the text aloud as students follow along. Model the use of expression to show how the characters' voices sound when they speak.	
	Reread to Clarify	• Have students reread the excerpt to clarify. Instruct them to circle words or portions of the text that need clarification. • Direct students to meet in pairs to discuss the text they circled along with strategies for clarifying them.	"At first, I wondered how a cloud of dust communicates to them that someone was coming. Then, as I visualized, I realized that a large group of people walking around will kick up dirt."
	Reread to Question	• Tell students to reread the text and brainstorm questions they would like to have answered about the text. Direct them to ask questions about the message of the text. Have students use sentence starters such as: I wonder..., How did..., Why did.... • Ask students to meet in pairs to share their questions and discuss answers.	"I wonder why the soldiers are called the *Invincibles*."
	Reread to Summarize and Respond	• Ask partners to work together to summarize the excerpt in one paragraph of four or five sentences. Then, have them act out pantomimes of portions of the text.	

*****Note:** For more tips, engagement strategies, and fluency options to include in this lesson, see pages 122–128.

Excerpt from *The Guns of Bull Run*

by Joseph A. Altsheler

Harry did fall asleep after a while. He awoke before dawn. He found that there was already bustle and movement in the army about him. Fires were lighted farther back. An early but plentiful breakfast was cooked. All were up and ready. The sun rose over the Virginia fields.

"Another hot day," said Happy Tom. "The sun is as red as fire! And look how it burns on the water there."

"Hot it will be," Harry said to himself. They had eaten their breakfast. Now they lay once more among the trees. Harry searched with his eyes the bushes and thickets on the other side. He looked for their riflemen. Most of them were still invisible in the day. Then, the Southern brigades were ordered to lie down. They lay there some time. Then, Harry felt that the film of dust on the edge of the wind was growing stronger. They saw a great cloud of it rising above hills and trees. It was moving toward them.

"They are coming," said St. Clair. "In less than a half hour, they will be at the ford."

"But I doubt if they know what is waiting for them," said Harry.

The cloud of dust rapidly came nearer. Now they heard the beat of horses' feet. They heard the clank of artillery. Harry began to breathe hard. He and the other young officers walked up and down the lines of their company. All the Invincibles clearly saw that great plume of dust. They heard the ominous sounds that came with it. It was very near now. Suddenly, the fringe of forest on the far side of the river burst into flame. The hidden riflemen had opened fire. They were burning the front of the advancing army.

But the Northern men came steadily on. They were rousing the riflemen out of the bushes. Then, they appeared among the trees on the north side of Bull Run. It was a New York brigade led by Tyler. The moment their faces showed, there was a tremendous discharge from the Southern batteries masked in the wood. The crash was appalling. Harry shut his eyes for a moment. He did it to shut out the horror. He saw the entire front rank of the Northern force go down. Then, the Southern sharpshooters opened with their rifles. There were hundreds who lined the water's edge. A storm of lead crashed into the ranks of the hapless New Yorkers.

"Up, Invincibles!" cried Colonel Talbot. They began to fire. They loaded. They fired again into the attacking force. The force had walked into what was almost an ambush.

"They will never reach the ford!" shouted Happy Tom.

"Never!" Harry shouted back.

Name: _____ Date: _____

Excerpt from *The Guns of Bull Run* Response

Directions: Reread the text on page 114 to answer each question.

1. Which of the following shows the author's use of figurative language?

   Ⓐ The cloud of dust rapidly came nearer.

   Ⓑ The crash was appalling.

   Ⓒ Look how it burns on the water there.

   Ⓓ The sun is as red as fire!

2. The text says that Harry starts to breathe hard. What does that communicate about how he feels?
   _____
   _____
   _____

3. Why does Harry close his eyes when the firing begins?
   _____
   _____
   _____
   _____

soldiers experiencing the thick of battle

Name:_____ Date:_____

Let's Compare!

Pearl Harbor vs. Bull Run

Directions: Reread both texts. Complete the chart, comparing the two events.

Pearl Harbor	Guns of Bull Run
Describe the setting before the attack.	**Describe the setting before the attack.**
How prepared were they?	**How prepared were they?**
What do we learn about the military men and women?	**What do we learn about the military men?**

Name: _____ Date: _____

Thinking About the Devastation of War

Directions: Choose at least two of these activities to complete.

Expanding Reading

Reread "Pearl Harbor" and "Bull Run." Research the lyrics to the songs "Battle Cry of Freedom" and "Remember Pearl Harbor." Then analyze how the songs are alike and how they are different.

Building Fluency

Imagine that you are creating a documentary about the bombing of Pearl Harbor. In pairs, assume the roles of reporters. Take turns reading paragraphs aloud, focusing on increasing voice intensity when telling about the attack. Add to the presentation by displaying photos from the Pearl Harbor attack in a presentation in the background.

Exploring Words

Review the excerpt from *The Guns at Bull Run*. Create a list of descriptive words and phrases used by the author and create illustrations to go with them.

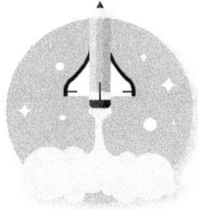

Crafting Writing

Imagine that you are Harry from *The Guns at Bull Run*. As you are having breakfast that morning, you decide to write a journal entry. Write about where you are and what you have experienced.

© Shell Education   51735—Close Reading with Paired Texts   117

References Cited

Brassel, Danny, and Timothy Rasinski. 2008. *Comprehension that Works: Taking Students Beyond Ordinary Understanding to Deep Comprehension.* Huntington Beach, CA: Shell Education.

Common Core State Standards Initiative. 2010. *Common Core State Standards for English Language Arts & Literacy in History/Social Studies, Science, and Technical Subjects.* Washington, DC: National Governors Association Center for Best Practices and the Council of Chief State School Officers.

Fisher, David, and Nancy Frey. 2012. "Close Reading in Elementary Schools." *The Reading Teacher* 66 (3): 179–188.

Hattie, John A. 2008. *Visible Learning: A Synthesis of Over 800 Meta-Analyses Relating to Achievement.* Oxford, UK: Routledge.

Oczkus, Lori D. 2018. *Reciprocal Teaching at Work: Powerful Strategies and Lessons for Improving Reading Comprehension 3rd Edition.* Virginia: ASCD.

Oczkus, Lori D. 2012. *Just the Facts!: Close Reading and Comprehension of Informational Text.* Huntington Beach, CA: Shell Education and International Reading Association (copublication).

Palincsar, Annemarie Sullivan, and Ann L. Brown. 1986. "Interactive Teaching to Promote Independent Learning from Text." *The Reading Teacher* 39 (8): 771–777.

Rasinski, Timothy V. 2010. *The Fluent Reader: Oral and Silent Reading Strategies for Building Fluency, Word Recognition and Comprehension 2nd Edition.* New York: Scholastic.

Rasinski, Timothy V., and Lorraine Griffith. 2010. *Building Fluency Through Practice and Performance.* Huntington Beach, CA: Shell Education.

Rasinski, Timothy V., and Melissa C. Smith. 2018. *Megabook of Fluency.* New York: Scholastic.

Rosenshine, Barak, and Carla Meister. 1994. "Reciprocal Teaching: A Review of the Research." *Review of Educational Research* 64 (4): 479–530.

Correlation to the Standards

Shell Education is committed to producing educational materials that are research and standards based. In this effort, we have correlated all of our products to the academic standards of all 50 states, the District of Columbia, the Department of Defense Dependents Schools, and all Canadian provinces. We have also correlated to TESOL, WIDA, and ISTE standards.

How to Find Standards Correlations

To print a customized correlation report of this product for your state, visit our website at **www.teachercreatedmaterials.com/administrators/correlations/** and follow the online directions. If you require assistance in printing correlation reports, please contact the Customer Service Department at 1-877-777-3450.

Purpose and Intent of Standards

The Every Student Succeeds Act (ESSA) mandates that all states adopt challenging academic standards that help students meet the goal of college and career readiness. While many states already adopted academic standards prior to ESSA, the act continues to hold states accountable for detailed and comprehensive standards.

Standards are designed to focus instruction and guide adoption of curricula. Standards are statements that describe the criteria necessary for students to meet specific academic goals. They define the knowledge, skills, and content students should acquire at each level. Standards are also used to develop standardized tests to evaluate students' academic progress. Teachers are required to demonstrate how their lessons meet state standards. State standards are used in the development of all of our products, so educators can be assured they meet the academic requirements of each state.

College and Career Readiness

Today's College and Career Readiness (CCR) standards offer guidelines for preparing K–12 students with the knowledge and skills that are necessary to succeed in postsecondary job training and education. CCR standards include the Common Core State Standards (CCSS) as well as other state-adopted standards like the Texas Essential Knowledge and Skills (TEKS) and the Virginia Standards of Learning (SOL).

McREL Compendium

Each year, McREL analyzes state standards and revises the compendium to produce a general compilation of national standards. The chart on page 121 lists the standards addressed in each lesson.

TESOL and WIDA Standards

The activities in this book promote English language development for English language learners. The chart on page 121 lists the standards addressed in each lesson.

ISTE Standards

The International Society for Technology in Education (ISTE) standards provide guidelines for the knowledge and skills needed to succeed in the twenty-first century.

Correlations to the Standards (cont.)

College and Career Readiness Standards	Lesson(s)
Analyze in detail how a key individual, event or idea is introduced, illustrated, and elaborated in a text (e.g., through examples or anecdotes).	Radiation (p. 73)
Cite specific textual evidence to support analysis of primary and secondary sources.	Beauty (p. 10)
Cite textual evidence to support analysis of what the text says explicitly as well as inferences drawn from the text.	Monster Movies (p. 28); Cryptography (p. 55); Equal Rights (p. 91)
Compare and contrast texts in different forms or genres (e.g., stories and poems; historical novels and fantasy stories) in terms of their approaches to similar themes and topics.	Equal Rights (p. 91)
Determine a central idea of a text and analyze its development over the course of the text, including how it emerges and is shaped and refined by specific details; provide an objective summary of the text.	Geometry (p. 37); Engineering and Technology (p. 64); Stress (p. 82); Women's Suffrage (p. 100); The Devastation of War (p. 109)
Determine a theme or central idea of a text and how it is conveyed through particular details; provide a summary of the text distinct from personal opinions or judgments.	Beauty (p. 10); Mark Twain (p. 19); Geometry (p. 37); Fractals (p. 46); Engineering and Technology (p. 64); Radiation (p.73); Stress (p. 82); The Devastation of War (p. 109)
Determine the meaning of words and phrases as they are used in a text, including figurative and connotative meanings; analyze the impact of a specific word choice on meaning and tone.	Fractals (p. 46); Cryptography (p. 55)
Engage effectively in a range of collaborative discussions.	Mark Twain (p. 19); Monster Movies (p. 28)
Write informative/explanatory texts to examine a topic and convey ideas, concepts, and information through the selection, organization, and analysis of relevant content.	Women's Suffrage (p. 100)
Determine the central ideas or information of a primary or secondary source; provide an accurate summary of the source distinct from prior knowledge or opinions.	Beauty (p. 10)

Correlations to the Standards (cont.)

McREL Standards	Lesson(s)
Analyze patterns and relationships.	Fractals (p. 46)
Draw, construct, and describe geometrical figures and describe the relationships between them.	Geometry (p. 37)
Understands that mathematics is the study of any pattern or relationship.	Cryptography (p. 55)
Understands major discoveries in science and medicine in the first half of the 20th century (e.g., those made by Curie, Einstein, Freud) and how they affected the quality of life and traditional views of nature, the cosmos, and the psyche	Radiation (p. 73)
Knows strategies to manage stress and feelings caused by disappointment, separation, or loss (e.g., talking over problems with others, understanding that feelings of isolation and depression will pass, examining the situation leading to the feelings)	Stress (p. 82)
Understands the struggle for racial and gender equality and for the extension of civil liberties	Equal Rights (p. 91); Women's Suffrage (p. 100)
Understands that war has an impact on shaping the United States.	The Devastation of War (p. 109)

TESOL/WIDA Standards	Lesson(s)
English language learners **communicate** for **social, intercultural, and instructional** purposes within the school setting	All lessons
English language learners **communicate** information, ideas, and concepts necessary for academic success in the area of **language arts**	All lessons
English language learners **communicate** information, ideas, and concepts necessary for academic success in the area of **mathematics**	All mathematics lessons
English language learners **communicate** information, ideas, and concepts necessary for academic success in the area of **science**	All science lessons
English language learners **communicate** information, ideas, and concepts necessary for academic success in the area of **social studies**	All social studies lessons

Tips for Implementing the Lessons

Lesson Tips

Below are additional tips and suggestions you may wish to do with students as you implement the lessons.

- Choose 4 to 6 words from each text pair and place them on a word wall for students to observe. Students can complete various word activities with the words.
- Use online resources, such as video clips or audio clips, to help students better understand the content.
- Have students research the authors of some of the texts or research more about the content in the texts so students can gain more knowledge.
- Keep a running list of strategies students use to clarify words, phrases, and ideas. Have the list visible for students to use as they clarify texts (e.g., reread, read on, sound out).
- Choose a long word from a text and present the letters of the word to students in alphabetical order, dividing the letters into consonants and vowels. Guide students to make a series of 5 to 10 words with the letters by giving them word meanings or clues to guess the words.
- Play WORDO with students by having them draw 4 x 4 matrixes. Display 16 to 20 words from the texts. Have students write one word in each box. Randomly select a word and call out its definition. Have each student mark the box the word is in. The first student to get four words in a straight or diagonal line calls out, "Wordo!"
- Invite students to act out words, sentences, or main ideas of a text with or without using their voices. Have the rest of the class guess what is being acted out.

Pacing Tips

Below are suggested options for implementing the lessons with students.

An Ideal Pacing Plan	If Working with Longer Texts
Day 1: Nonfiction text close reading lesson/follow-up activities **Day 2:** Fiction text close reading lesson/follow-up activities **Day 3:** Compare the texts/follow-up activities **Day 4:** Reread texts/follow-up activities **Day 5:** Reread texts/share follow-up activities	**Day 1:** Complete the close reading steps, including predicting, clarifying, questioning, and summarizing, for the first portion of the text. **Day 2:** Run through all four steps again for the second portion of the text. **Note:** The follow-up activities should be done at the conclusion of the entire reading of a text.

Strategies

Engagement Strategies

Make learning memorable by using the following engagement strategies.

Discussion in Pairs

Throughout the lessons, have students talk with partners or groups to enhance comprehension. Conduct whole-group sharing after partners discuss their responses.

Mark or Code with Text Symbols

Have students work independently or in groups to mark the text using symbols to show their thinking. Provide copies of the text for students and page 126 for students to use as they annotate the text while they read. Symbols may include:

❑ main idea   ★ details   ? confused   ↔ connection

Have students use different colored pencils, highlighters, or markers as they read.

Discussion Sentence Frames

Have students use discussion sentence frames when sharing responses with others. Frames help keep students on task during discussions. Some examples include:

Predict I think I will learn ____ because____. I think the author wrote this because ____.	**Clarify** I didn't get the word/sentence ____, so I ____.
Question Who, what, when, where, why, how, I wonder ____.	**Summarize** This is about ____. The main idea is ____.

Close Reading Props

Bring in a pair of goofy glasses or a magnifying glass to hold up when it is time to read a text closely.

Glasses	**Magnifying Glass**
Tell students, "Close reading is like putting on special glasses as you reread the text to figure it out."	Tell students, "Close reading is like using a magnifying glass to help you understand the text as you reread it."

Sing to the Strategies

Help students remember the different purposes for rereading by creating a song with verses for each of the reciprocal teaching strategies. A song option can be found on page 128.

Strategies (cont)

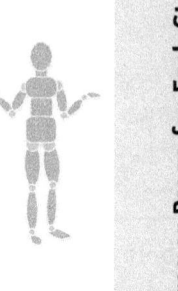

Gestures or Props for Each Strategy

Use gestures or props to help students remember the close reading strategies as they closely read a text.

Predict: Use a physical crystal ball, or pretend to rub a crystal ball to predict what will happen or what the text is about using clues from the text.	**Question:** Use a physical microphone, or use a fist to make a microphone to interview one another asking and answering questions.
Clarify: Use glasses or a magnifying glass. You can also use your arms: parallel to show a "pause" button, to point to the left for rewind, and to the right for reading on to help clarify tricky words in a text.	**Summarize:** Use a lasso (with yarn or string), or pretend to wield a lasso to rope in the "main ideas and details" of a text.

Adapted from Lori Oczkus (2018)

Fluency Strategies

The chart below lists various fluency techniques to use with students.

Model Fluent Reading	Have a proficient reader read the text to students. After the reading, teacher leads students in a discussion of the content of the text *and* the way in which the teacher or reader reads the text (e.g., expression, phrasing, pacing).
Assisted Reading— Choral Reading	Have groups of students read the text orally. Students who are more fluent readers provide an assist to students who are less fluent.
Assisted Reading— Paired Reading	Ask two readers to read a text orally together. One reader is more proficient than the other. The more proficient reader acts as a model for the less fluent one.
Assisted Reading— Audio-recorded Reading	Have a student read a text while at the same time listening to a fluent recording of the same text. The recorded reading acts as a model for the student.
Assisted Reading— Echo Reading	Teacher reads the text aloud while tracking the print for students to see. After the text has been read aloud, children imitate, or echo, the teacher as they visually track the text.
Repeated Reading	Have students read a text several times orally and silently for different purposes. One purpose for rereading is to improve students' fluency (e.g., word recognition, automaticity, and expression).
Phrased Text Reading	The teacher or student marks the appropriate phrase boundaries in a text with slash marks. The student then reads the text, pausing at the marked locations. Readers who lack fluency often read in a word-by-word manner that limits the meaning of the passage. These visual cues give students support in reading in meaningful phrases.

Adapted from Timothy Rasinski (2010)

Assessment Options

Aside from students' work on the activity pages, there are many opportunities to assess students during each step of the close reading process. Use the chart below to guide your assessments.

Ready, Set, Predict!

Does the student . . .
- skim the text/visuals to make logical predictions?
- relate relevant prior knowledge?
- anticipate author's purpose?
- predict topic/theme?
- anticipate how the text is organized?

Go!

Does the student . . .
- make an attempt to read the text independently?
- follow along during the teacher read-aloud?
- mark unfamiliar words and ideas?
- participate in shared readings; follow along?
- identify what makes the teacher's reading fluent?

Reread to Clarify

Does the student . . .
- reread to mark words they want to know or clarify?
- identify words/lines that help students visualize?
- identify more than one "fix it" strategy such as sounding out, chopping words into parts, rereading, reading on?

Reread to Question

Does the student . . .
- reread to ask or create questions for peers?
- reread to answer text-dependent questions using text evidence?
- confidently ask and answer questions?

Reread to Summarize and Respond

Does the student . . .
- select main ideas and details to summarize?
- summarize selection in order?
- use key vocabulary to summarize?
- mark text to show responses using symbols?

   ❑ main idea   ★ details   ? confused   ↔ connection

- compare/contrast the fiction and nonfiction texts?

Annotation Chart

Directions: Use the following symbols to annotate the text while you read.

☆	Important detail
☐	Main idea
?	I don't understand
↔	I made a connection
!	I'm surprised

Close Reading Bookmarks

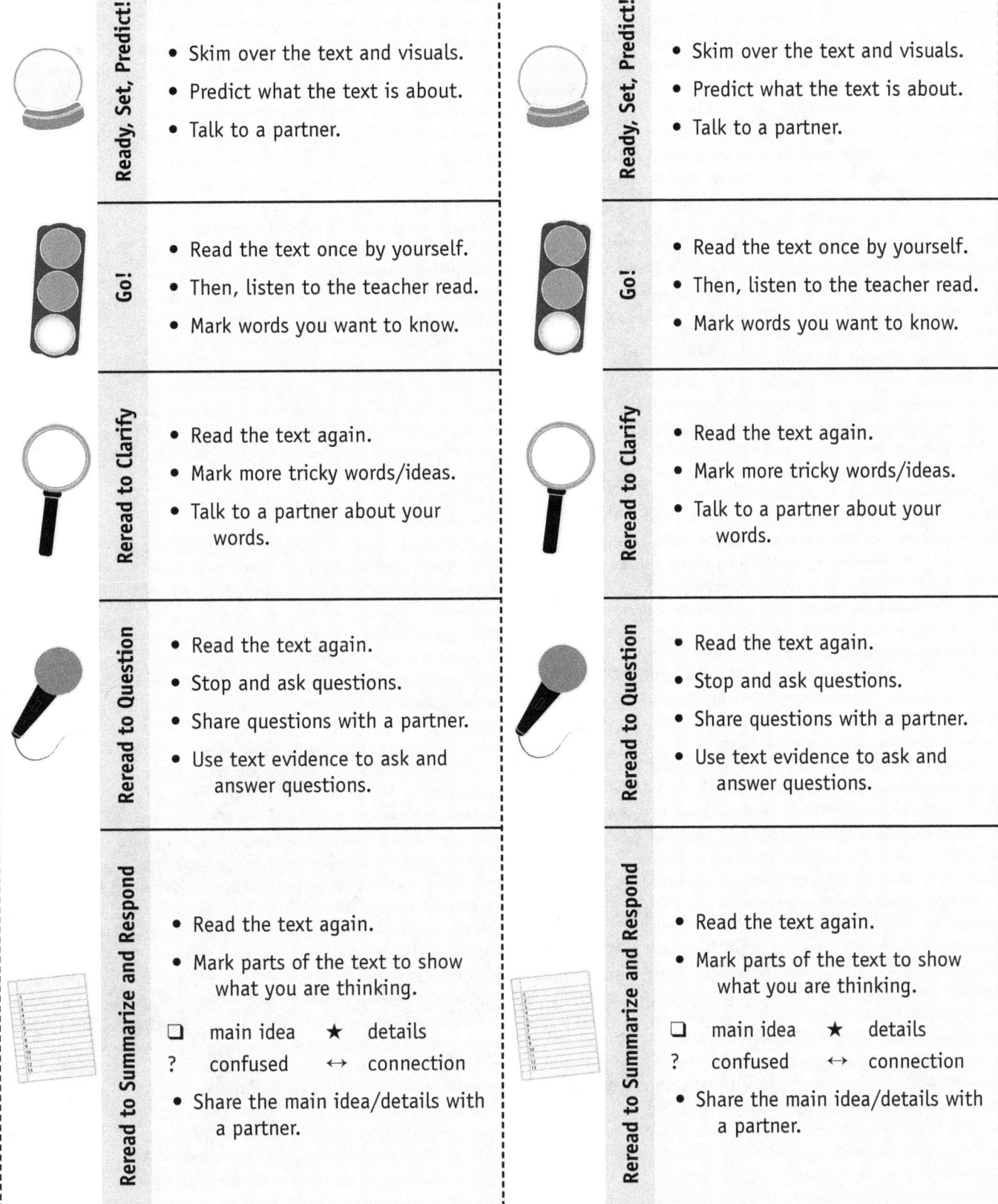

Ready, Set, Predict!
- Skim over the text and visuals.
- Predict what the text is about.
- Talk to a partner.

Go!
- Read the text once by yourself.
- Then, listen to the teacher read.
- Mark words you want to know.

Reread to Clarify
- Read the text again.
- Mark more tricky words/ideas.
- Talk to a partner about your words.

Reread to Question
- Read the text again.
- Stop and ask questions.
- Share questions with a partner.
- Use text evidence to ask and answer questions.

Reread to Summarize and Respond
- Read the text again.
- Mark parts of the text to show what you are thinking.
  - ☐ main idea   ★ details
  - ? confused   ↔ connection
- Share the main idea/details with a partner.

Read it Again: Sure to Win!

Lyrics by Timothy Rasinski

(Sung to the tune of "Take Me Out To The Ball Game")

Here's a tip for your reading—
Here's a tip: prediction!
Skim through the passage now, more or less,
Then you can form a pretty good guess!
Then, it's read, read, read through the passage;
Did your prediction come true?
Read it once, twice, maybe three times
To make sense to you!

Here's a tip for your reading—
Here's a tip: read again!
Hard words and tricky parts you may spy,
Read it once more to help clarify!
So, just read, read, read through your passage.
You're sure to win if you do!
Read it once, twice, maybe three times
To make sense to you!

Here's a tip for your reading—
Here's a tip: read again!
Read it, and then you a question ask;
Look to the text to help in this task!
So, just read, read, read through your passage,
You're sure to win if you do!
Read it once, twice, maybe three times
To make sense to you!

Here's a tip for your reading—
Here's a tip: read again!
Then read it once more to summarize
All the main parts are before your eyes.
So, just read, read, read through your passage,
You're sure to win if you do!
Read it once, twice, maybe three times
To make sense to you!